Cuban Elegance

Cuban Elegance

MICHAEL CONNORS

Michael Connors (signature)

PHOTOGRAPHS BY BRUCE BUCK

HARRY N. ABRAMS, INC., PUBLISHERS

CONTENTS

PAGE 1: A PAIR OF EARLY-NINE-
TEENTH-CENTURY MAHOGANY
AND CANE HIGH-BACK ARM-
CHAIRS MADE IN CUBA'S COLO-
NIAL CITY OF MATANZAS
PAGE 2: ONE OF THE MANY
BEAUTIFUL WOMEN OF CUBA
PAGE 3: A NUMBER OF PRIVATE
HOMES IN CUBA TODAY DISPLAY
COLONIAL FURNITURE.
OPPOSITE: RENAISSANCE-
REVIVAL ISLAND FURNITURE
IN A PRIVATE HOME IN RURAL
CUBA, WHERE TRAVEL BY
HORSE IS STILL COMMON

DEDICATION

This book is dedicated to Fundación Amistad, a nonprofit organization whose mission is to foster mutual understanding and respect between the peoples of the United States and Cuba.

To advance this mission, Fundación Amistad sponsors educational exchanges and programs, research projects, and community outreach initiatives, which deepen the American and Cuban peoples' knowledge and appreciation of each other's culture, history, and society.

FIG. 1. A NINETEENTH-CENTURY CUBAN-MADE HUMIDOR OF EXOTIC INDIGENOUS WOODS, MADE FOR THE FAMOUS H. UPMAN COMPANY

PREFACE

With over five hundred years of written history, the island of Cuba has the oldest colonial heritage in the Western Hemisphere. Part of this heritage is Cuba's furniture, an art whose traditional forms help define the island's distinctive cultural essence, or *Cubanidad*. Although time has taken its toll, thousands of pieces remain from the four hundred years of Cuba's colonial period. Unfortunately, aside from the surviving examples themselves, sources of primary and secondary information about early Cuban furniture, including documented provenances, are rare. However, there are many dedicated and qualified historians, conservators, researchers, and curators who realize that as scholars of material culture they are the custodians for this irreplaceable patrimony. They know that the furniture existed long before they arrived on this earth, and that with care, it will exist long after they depart. It is their job to research, identify, describe, conserve, and steward this valuable part of Cuba's heritage. This book honors the people who, in the past, present, and in the future, have preserved and will continue to preserve this important and integral part of Cuba's history.

INTRODUCTION

For centuries the paradisiacal island of Cuba, the "Pearl of the Antilles," evoked a seductive and exotic image of riches, mystery, and pleasure. Cuba's natural beauty, history, architecture, art, people, and music are all part of the fabulous myth of the island.

Cuba, the largest island in the Caribbean Sea, was inhabited by the peaceful Tainos when Christopher Columbus arrived in 1492. Insisting that he had reached the Far East, Columbus wrote, "Never have human eyes beheld anything so beautiful," and he named the indigenous island people "Indians," an appellation that has survived to this day to describe the people of the West Indies. It was two years later that the Vatican—through a Papal Bull—divided the New World between Spain and Portugal. Spain's colonization of Cuba and the greater Antilles led to the conquest of Mexico and South America, with the exception of Brazil, which Pedralvarez Cabral claimed for Portugal in 1500. The establishment of "Nueva España" created unprecedented power and wealth for Spain. Her possessions in the Caribbean soon incited envy among the other countries of Europe, and her ownership of the islands did not go unchallenged for long. England, the United Netherlands, France, and Denmark all entered into a state of perpetual warfare with Spain, and with each other, over Spain's colonial claims and their own new settlements in the West Indies.

Fig. 2. "Isola Cuba," by the Venetian cartographer Vincenzo Coronelli, 1692

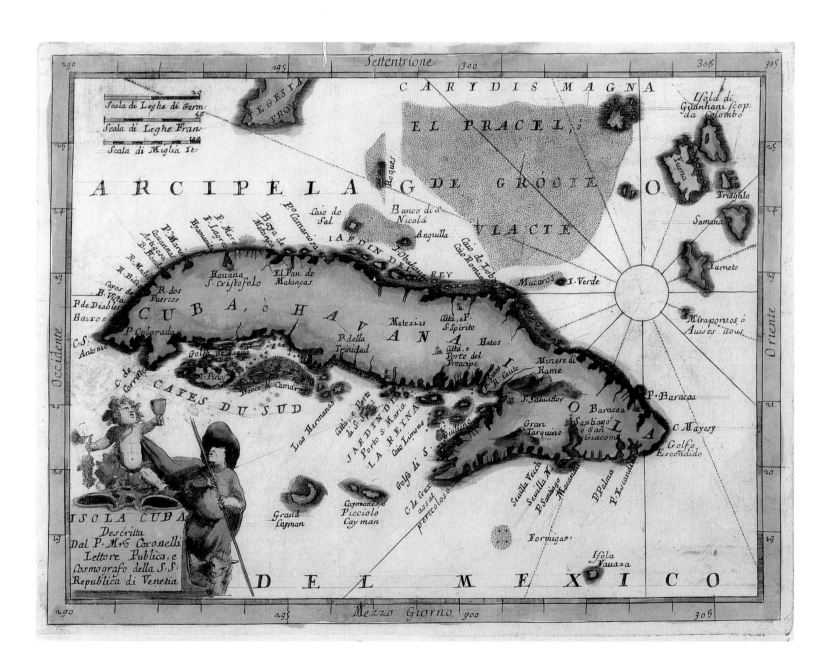

Settentrione

CARYDIS MAGNA

Scala di Leghe di Germ:
Scala di Leghe Fran:
Scala di Miglia It:

Isola di
Guanhani scop:
da Colombo

EL PRACEL;

ARCIPELA G DE GROOTE O

Yuma

Triagulo

Caio do
Sal

Banco di S.
Nicolà

VLACTE

Samana

P.o Camariora

P.o Maria
Guadiana
Artigosa
B. Honda

F. Moro
F. Lagrica
Buamici

Bya de
Matanças

JARDIN DEL

Anguilla

Caio de Iab.
Caio Romano

Turneto

R. Medio

R. dos
Puercos

Havana
S. Cristofolo

El Pan de
Matanças

REY

Mucaras

I. Verde

Cayos de
B. Vista
P. de Diables
Bairos

R. Blac

P. Colorado

CUBA, ò HAV

Misterias

A N

Citta, e P.
S. Spirito

Miraportos ó
Auises uous

C. S.
Antonio

P. della
Trinidad

Golfo de Xagua

C. de
Corrales

I. Pinos

Banco di Camar.

Hatos
Citta, e
Porto del
Prencipe

Minere di
Rame

R. Caute

Oriente

CAYES DU SUD

Las Hermanas

Citta, e Porto
di S. Jago

JARDIN DEL
Porto S. Maria
LA REYNA

S. Saluador

I

O Baracoa

P. Baracoa

C. Mayesy

Caio Limons

Giuliano

Gran
Tarquino

Santiago
o San
Giacom.

L A

Golfo
Escondido

Golfo di S.

C. de Gru
assa
pericoloso

Sevilla Vech.
Sevilla N.
P. Santiago

Macanan

P. Palma
P. Escandes

Grand
Cayman

Caymanes, o
Picciolo
Cayman

Formigas

ISOLA CUBA
Descritta
Dal P. M.o Coronelli
Lettore Publica, e
Cosmografo della S. S.
Republica di Venetia

Isola
Nauaza

DEL MEXICO

Mezzo Giorno

Spain soon realized that Cuba was invaluable, not for the gold and silver that Columbus had anticipated, but for its geopolitical position as a strategic stepping-stone for the newly discovered territories of Mexico and Peru; Cuba was truly the "key to the New World."

Spain's dominance in the West Indies lasted just sixty years, until 1555, when Havana, then known as San Cristóbal, was attacked and sacked by French buccaneer Jacques de Sores. Cuban forts, modeled after Medieval and Renaissance designs, were erected after the attack; and, as foreign incursions increased, more fortifications were constructed. Havana's oldest existing building and the New World's second oldest fort, called La Fuerza, was begun in the late 1550s by architect Bartolomé Sánchez. Havana's commander, or *capitán general,* resided at La Fuerza until 1762. In 1589, two more forts, La Punta and El Morro, were built on opposite sides of the Havana harbor for protection. By the turn of the seventeenth century, Havana was established as Spain's colonial capital and had a population of nearly 10,000. Cuba was not only the Caribbean's major commercial trading port but also the assembly point for Spain's ships—which carried cargoes of soldiers, arms, and provisions from Europe—as well as for the treasure fleets from Peru and Mexico laden with gold and silver. By the mid-sixteenth century, Spanish galleons, loaded with such Chinese treasures as silk, porcelain, pearls, and ivory, came to port at Acapulco, on the Pacific coast of Mexico, and from there were carried overland and loaded again onto ships bound for Spain by way of Cuba.

Many of these riches were shipped back to Seville, Columbus's departure point; Seville was therefore the largest, richest, and the most important port of departure for the Americas. As a result, many of the first colonists emigrated from this region, Spain's southern province of Andalusia, on the Guadalquivir River. Among these early colonists were shipwrights, housewrights, masons, blacksmiths, and stonecutters, who had basic knowledge of architecture, carpentry, and shipbuilding. Because these individuals were probably more concerned with survival than crafting furniture designed for comfort or decorative ornamentation, the first furnishings made on Cuba were rustic and primitive, consisting of the bare essentials only.

military transport and the treasure fleets that brought gold and silver from Mexico and Peru.

By the middle of the sixteenth century, Cuba's gold rush had abated, and the colonists began to turn to agriculture. Tobacco, sugar, and coffee became key exports. As the colony continued to grow, aristocratic colonial residences were modeled after Spanish examples, in architectural styles imported from Spain. Furniture imported from Spain began to be replaced and replicated by local craftsmen; many of these pieces exhibited the recognizable Arabian features of the Mudéjar style that was fashionable during the period. A piece of furniture is classified as Mudéjar when it employs traditional craft techniques that emerged in Spain during Islamic rule and was used by Christians after the region was reconquered by the Spanish.[1]

These first pieces of Cuban furniture were Renaissance forms such as the trunk or chest, the most common and most useful piece of furniture; *sillones fraileros* or "friars' chairs," sometimes called "monks' chairs"; armoires; and *vargueños,* or writing desks.

During the seventeenth century, buildings were constructed in the palatial and highly ornamented Spanish colonial Plateresque style, which was derived from Spain's elaborately decorated Renaissance and late Gothic architecture. Changes in furniture styles were also typically catalyzed by both Spanish and foreign influences. For example, the English occupied Cuba in 1762 until the Treaty of Paris returned the island to Spain in exchange for Florida the following year. During the English occupation and thereafter, Cuban furniture forms and styles became noticeably more Georgian in appearance. Later in the eighteenth century, the Rococo style was imported from France and furniture again took on a different look.

During the eighteenth century, Cuba came into its own. It was no longer just a springboard for treasure-laden Spanish galleons returning to Europe, but a wealthy agricultural center producing tobacco, cotton, and especially, sugar. It was sugar, *oro dulce,* or "sweet gold," that brought untold wealth, prosperity, and a plutocracy of plantation society to Cuba. The last half of the eighteenth and early nineteenth centuries represented

OPPOSITE:
FIG. 6. CARTS SIMILAR TO THIS ONE HAVE BEEN USED IN CUBA SINCE EARLY COLONIAL DAYS.

LEFT:
FIG. 7. FIELDS OF TOBACCO IN THE WESTERN PROVINCE OF PINAR DEL RIO

BELOW:
FIG. 8. THE HARVEST NEAR VUELTA ABAJO, THE HOME OF CUBA'S WORLD-FAMOUS TOBACCO, LASTS FROM JANUARY TO THE END OF MARCH.

FIG. 9. SPANIARDS CALLED
THIS CHAIR FORM A *FRAILERO*,
A MONASTIC OR MONK'S CHAIR.
THIS SEVENTEENTH-CENTURY
CUBAN VERSION IS TYPICAL OF
THE ONES CRAFTED IN CUBA
FROM THE FIFTEENTH TO THE
NINETEENTH CENTURY.

FIG. 10. ONE OF THE MANY
SIXTEENTH- AND SEVEN-
TEENTH-CENTURY CEDAR
CHESTS FOUND THROUGHOUT
CUBA AND THE CARIBBEAN.
THE MUDÉJAR STEP-PROFILE
DOVETAILS DISTINGUISH IT AS
CUBAN-MADE.

FIG. 11. DETAIL OF THE
WOODEN CEILING IN THE
CASA DE DIEGO VELÁZQUEZ IN
SANTIAGO DE CUBA. THE
CEILING EXEMPLIFIES THE
SPANISH MUDÉJAR STYLE THAT
PREDOMINATED IN CUBAN
ARCHITECTURE AT THE BEGIN-
NING OF THE COLONIAL
PERIOD.

FIG. 12. SEVENTEENTH-
CENTURY ARMOIRES SIMILAR
TO THIS CUBAN ONE WERE
CRAFTED FROM ISLAND
CEDAR.

FIG. 13. A CUBAN VERSION
OF THE SPANISH *VARGUEÑO*
CABINET. THE MOST CHARAC-
TERISTIC PIECE OF SPANISH
FURNITURE, THIS SIXTEENTH-
CENTURY EXAMPLE WOULD
BE MORE CORRECTLY CALLED
A *PAPELERA* BECAUSE IT DOES
NOT HAVE A FALL FRONT OR
DOORS.

FIG. 14. DETAIL OF A CUBAN
CARVED BALL-AND-CLAW FOOT
ON AN EARLY EIGHTEENTH-
CENTURY ARMOIRE INFLU-
ENCED BY ENGLISH STYLE

FIG. 15. DECORATIVE MOTIFS
CARVED ON DOORS AND WIN-
DOWS WERE ALSO CARVED ON
ARMOIRES, OFTEN BY THE
SAME CRAFTSMEN.

the height of the island's prosperity, a period of foreign fashion and design influence, and a time when the most luxurious furnishings enhanced Cuban life.

Through the nineteenth century, Cuban furniture went through a variety of artistic styles—including neoclassicism and the revival styles—and was alternately influenced by Spain, England, France, and North America. Over the colonial period, the evolution of Cuban furniture was affected by a variety of influences, including the example of imported models, the ingenuity of native and immigrant craftsmen, the island's tropical climate, and economic fluctuation. At the end of the century, with the Spanish-American War, Cuba's life as a colony culminated in independence and four hundred years of colonial Cuban furniture ended.

Cuba's colonial cabinetmakers discovered unique and distinctive decorative motifs as well as entire expressions of forms. Although Cuban furniture-makers remained anonymous during the colonial period, there were exceptions during the nineteenth century. That period also saw the industrial revolution and the development of machines capable of mass-producing furniture at lower prices, some of which were labeled by the manufacturer. The demand for master craftsmanship lessened and cabinetmakers lost patronage and the representative symbols of luxury. Ostentation had come full circle as the wealthiest families of the Spanish Antilles began once again importing what was considered more luxurious furniture from abroad.

With the exception of the few nineteenth-century labeled pieces there are no signed examples of Cuban colonial furniture; therefore when a historian seeks to trace and establish an identity for colonial furniture forms he must not be confined by any preconceived paradigm but must allow one discovery to lead to another, eventually finding the origin or provenance of the form (or often simply stumbling onto it). In Cuba, the use of the native tropical hardwoods, skillful craftsmanship, original decorative elements, construction techniques, and indigenous furniture designs were identifying elements found throughout the truly unique cultural patrimony of colonial Cuban furniture left to us today.

FIG. 19. THIS CUBAN ROCOCO-REVIVAL MAHOGANY ARMOIRE IS TYPICAL OF ISLAND FURNITURE COPIED AFTER MACHINE-MADE REVIVAL PIECES IMPORTED FROM EUROPE AND NORTH AMERICA.

OPPOSITE:

FIG. 20. AN EXAMPLE OF THE
OPULENT FURNITURE AND
DECORATIONS TO BE FOUND IN
A LATE SEVENTEENTH- OR
EARLY EIGHTEENTH-CENTURY
CUBAN *PALACIO*

FIG. 21. A COLLECTION OF
CUBAN HAND-CARVED AND
POLYCHROMED WOOD CRUCI-
FIXION FIGURES FROM THE
EIGHTEENTH AND NINE-
TEENTH CENTURIES

Chapter I DISCOVERY: THE SIXTEENTH CENTURY

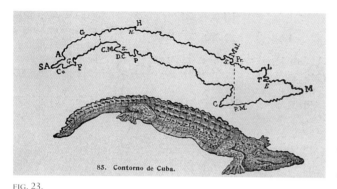

85. Contorno de Cuba.

FIG. 23.

It was Spain's greed for the riches and splendor of the Far East that Marco Polo had described two centuries earlier that led the explorer Christopher Columbus to discover the island of Cuba in 1492. Marco Polo had spent twenty years in Cathay (China) at the resplendent court of Kublai Khan and spoke of treasures "beyond belief": gold, silver, precious and semiprecious stones. He also mentioned the magnificently exotic land of Cypango, Polo's name for Japan.

Thanks to Columbus's journals and his letters to the Spanish sovereigns Ferdinand and Isabella, we have records not only of the discovery but of the wonders that befell these early explorers. After making landfall on October 12, 1492, in what is known today as the Bahamas, Columbus wrote in his log, "I wish to go and see if I can make the island of Cypango." Columbus never doubted that he was very near the fabulous fortunes of the Far East. He further recorded, "Following this I wish to leave for another very large island, which I believe must be Cypango, according to the signs these Indians who I have with me make. They call it Colba." Columbus misunderstood the Arawak name for the island, and misspelled it in his log entry as Cuba. Columbus's reference to Cypango confirmed that he believed that this new-found territory was a part of Asia, the treasure-rich land described by Marco Polo.[2]

When Columbus discovered Cuba, he named it Juana after the daughter of King Ferdinand and Queen Isabella. The natives, who believed the island was shaped like a crocodile (see fig. 23), continued to call the island Colba. The largest island in the Caribbean Sea, Cuba is part of the West Indian chain of islands originally called the Caribe Islands (named for the cannibalistic Caribs who populated most of the islands south of Cuba). The Spanish divided the chain into groups: the Greater (the northern group) and the Lesser (southern group) Antilles, both of which were named after Antilla, a mythical land that was believed to exist east of the Azores. Cuba is nearly 43,000 square miles, approximately 780 miles from end to end and 125 miles at its widest point. It comprises over 1,600 cays (low coral banks) and islands. Describing the newly discovered land as an "earthly paradise," Columbus went on to write:

> *I have never seen a more beautiful place. Along the banks of the river were trees I have never seen at home, with flowers and fruit of the most diverse kinds, among the branches of which one heard the delightful chirping of birds. There were a great number of palms. When I descended from the launch, I approached two fishermen's huts. Upon seeing me, the natives took fright and fled. Back on the boat, I went up the river for a good distance. I felt such joy upon seeing these flowery gardens and green forests and hearing the birds sing that I could not tear myself away, and thus continued my trip. This island is truly the most beautiful land human eyes have ever beheld.*[3]

Cuba's earliest inhabitants were the Ciboney, who probably arrived from Florida around 4,000 BC. Later (around 1,000 AD), the Arawak Tainos migrated from South America via the island of Hispaniola. Columbus described the indigenous Cubans as

> *So lovable, so tractable, so peaceful are these people that I swear to your majesties that there is not in the world a better nation nor a better land. They love their neighbors as themselves and their discourse is ever sweet and gentle and accompanied with a smile.*[4]

FIG. 24. A SIXTEENTH-CENTURY
EXAMPLE OF THE TYPICAL
CUBAN *TABURETE* CHAIR,
MADE OF ISLAND TROPICAL
HARDWOOD WITH A LEATHER
SEAT AND BACK-REST. THIS
SIMPLE FORM WAS AN INDIS-
PENSABLE PIECE OF FURNI-
TURE THROUGHOUT CUBA'S
COLONIAL PERIOD.

FIG. 25. A CUBAN-MADE SIX-
TEENTH-CENTURY MAHOGANY
BENCH. THE BACK-SLAT IS
SCALLOPED ON UPPER AND
LOWER EDGES, AND HAS A
RELIGIOUS CARVING AT ITS
CENTER. THE PRIMITIVE
CONSTRUCTION, TYPICAL OF
THE PERIOD, INCLUDES
STRAIGHT ARMS ENDING IN
MODIFIED SCROLLS AND LOW,
MORTISED STRETCHERS THAT
JOIN THE LEGS IN A BOX-LIKE
ENCLOSURE.

Two years after Columbus's discovery, and after lobbying from both the Catholic countries of Spain and Portugal, Pope Alexander VI issued a papal partition, the Treaty of
Tordesillas. This treaty established an imaginary line of division 270 leagues west of the
Cape Verde Islands which decreed Brazil to Portugal and the islands of the Caribbean and
all lands west to Spain on the condition that the gospel be spread and the natives be con-
verted to Christianity. After the declaration, Spain claimed and considered all the newly
discovered territories theirs, to rule as they pleased. And rule they did; they pursued their
destiny with a vengeance. Armed with the "cross and sword," Spain created an empire.

It wasn't until the early sixteenth century that colonization began. Contrary to Columbus's
theory that Cuba was part of Asia, in 1508 Sebastián de Ocampo discovered that Cuba was
an independent island. The first settlers arrived on the island with conquistador Diego

Velázquez de Cuellar in 1511. Velázquez had been lieutenant governor of the neighboring island Hispaniola, and according to historians J. H. Parry and P. M. Sherlock, "Velázquez was a disciplinarian and an administrator of considerable ability. With a small force of personal followers he put down native resistance and occupied the whole island— or at least, desirable sites throughout the island— within three years."[5]

By the end of the first quarter of the sixteenth century, Velázquez had founded Cuba's first seven towns: Baracoa, Santiago de Cuba, Bayamo, Sancti Spiritus, Puerto Principe, Trinidad, and Havana. He also established the *repartimiento* and *encomienda* systems of exploiting the indigenous population, which allowed the Spanish colonists to use the natives as servants, plantation laborers, and mine workers. The combination of these two systems, along with forced conversion to Christianity, resulted in the native population's genocide.

Bartolomé de las Casas, known as the "Protector of the Indians," was a priest who participated in Velázquez's campaigns; he was also Cuban history's most important witness to the period. In his diary he wrote:

The Indians came to meete us, and to receive us with victuals, and delicate cheere…. The Devill put himselfe into the Spaniards, to put them all to the edge of the sword in my presence, without any course whatsoever, more than three thousand soules, which were set before us men, women and children. I saw there so great cruelties, that never any man living either have or shall see the like.[6]

Although Las Casas was an ordained priest and crusaded against the massacre of Arawak Tainos, like his fellow colonists he accepted a grant both of *repartimiento* and *encomienda* and grew wealthy. He ultimately renounced his grants and fought to end the evils of the two systems.

FIG. 26. TYPICAL OF THE BAROQUE PERIOD THAT PRODUCED MORE FANCIFUL FORMS IN FURNITURE, THIS LATE SEVENTEENTH-CENTURY CUBAN VERSION OF THE *FRAILERO*, OR MONK'S CHAIR, HAS CURVILINEAR LINES AND AN UPHOLSTERED LEATHER SEAT AND BACK.

FIG. 27. A CUBAN MUDÉJAR-STYLE ARMOIRE, OR *ARMORIO*. THIS EARLY SEVENTEENTH-CENTURY CEDAR EXAMPLE IS TYPICAL OF SIXTEENTH- AND SEVENTEENTH-CENTURY *ARTESONADO* CONSTRUCTION.

BELOW:
FIG. 28. A CUBAN BAROQUE COF-
FER WITH A DOME LID AND IRON
LOCK-PLATES, DECORATED WITH
INCISED SCROLLING PATTERNS

FIG. 29. A NINETEENTH-CENTURY
COPY OF A SEVENTEENTH-CENTURY
SPANISH IRON STOOL, WITH SPHER-
ICAL BRASS HAND-SUPPORTS AND
AN IRON CURULE-FORM BASE.

OPPOSITE:
FIG. 30. THE PRIVATE DISPATCH
ROOM IN THE PALACIO DE LOS
CAPITANES GENERALES DISPLAYS A
COLLECTION OF LATE SIXTEENTH-,
SEVENTEENTH-, AND EARLY EIGH-
TEENTH-CENTURY FURNITURE.

Throughout the sixteenth century, the slaugh-
ter of the Amerindians and Spain's quest for gold
and silver continued. A Spanish historian wrote in
1587 that the treasure that entered Spain from the
New World was abundant enough to pave the streets
of Seville with blocks of gold and silver.[7] During
the sixteenth century, the supply of precious metals
in the Spanish Caribbean islands—especially in
Cuba—was dwindling to a trickle. To the Spanish,
Mexico and Peru were far more important because of
their huge gold and silver deposits; but strategically,
Cuba was still essential to Spain as a defensive bastion for
the colonies and for their treasure fleets' shipping routes.

Although by the sixteenth century's end, Cuba's production of
precious metals had abated, its tobacco and sugar farming had
begun to prosper, owing to the island's large land mass with its relatively few mountains and its very fertile soil. The success of Cuba's
agriculture not only sustained the island's population but also assured
goods for export, both to Spain and to her other new colonies. It was in
this period that Cuban buildings began to take on the distinct look of
her colonial interpretation of Renaissance style.

Sixteenth-century architects and engineers were given strict
instructions from the Spanish crown regarding the organization
and planning of the colonial settlements. Following the dictates
of Phillip II, who promulgated the "Law of the Indies" in 1573,
streets were arranged in grid formation at right angles to one
another. As one historian notes,

*The New Laws of the Indies actually derived from the theological
debate and were in theory intended to correct the moral transgres-
sions associated with colonization, thus protecting the rights of*

FIG. 31. THE DRAWING ROOM
OF THE CASA DE DIEGO
VELÁZQUEZ WITH ITS CHAR-
ACTERISTIC CUBAN *ALFARJE*
CEILING CARVED FROM
FRAGRANT ISLAND CEDAR-
WOOD

OPPOSITE:
FIG. 32. A PAIR OF SPANISH
RENAISSANCE-STYLE CUBAN
ARMCHAIRS WITH ELABO-
RATELY CARVED CRESTRAILS
THAT CENTER AN IMPORTED
SPANISH BAROQUE IVORY AND
EBONIZED CABINET ON STAND

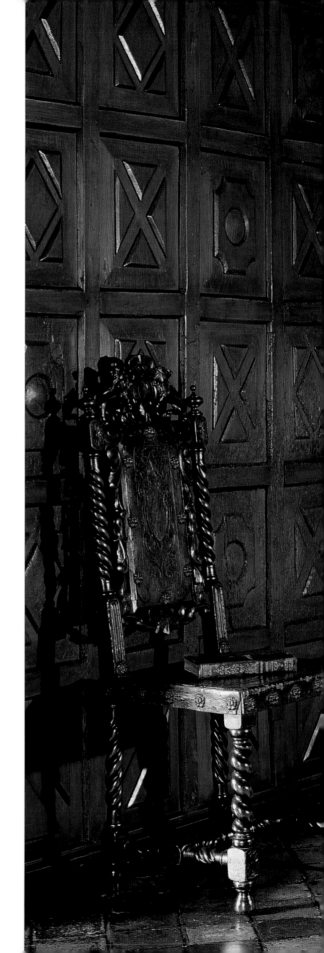

FIG. 33. AN EARLY PHOTO-
GRAPH OF TRINIDAD'S
CENTRAL TOWN PLAZA, A
COMMUNITY GATHERING
PLACE AND INTEGRAL PART
OF CUBA'S COLONIAL
URBAN LIFE

native populations. In practice, however, they served as an instrument of the state to control nearly every aspect of colonial life.[8]

The Spanish crown deployed European (mostly Spanish) military engineer-architects to design and develop Cuba's buildings. The centrally located main square was always bordered by a church or cathedral on one side, while the government office, military headquarters, and barracks flanked the other three sides. There were exceptions to this prescribed architectural design. For example, Havana was laid out with three different squares: an ecclesiastical square, a military square, and a governmental administrative square.

The architecture built during Cuba's first century of Spanish rule followed closely the different styles current in the mother country at the time, although buildings were modified for the island's tropical climate. Architecture derived from the styles of Spain's Mediterranean coast —whether Arab, Roman, or Spanish—contributed to an amalgamation of styles in Cuba. The patio, for instance, with its origins in ancient Roman as well as Arab construction, appeared frequently in wealthy Cuban residences. In the 1500s there was no one predominant style of architecture in Spain. Indeed,

> *Spanish Renaissance architecture cannot be thought of as showing a unified style or coherent development common to all regions in the sixteenth century. Not only did Gothic elements persist in modified forms into the sixteenth century (as did some simple traditional forms, such as Mudéjar, in the south of the country), but there was also great local variation in the degree of acceptance of and resistance to stylistic innovation.*[9]

Consequently, the new settlements and towns of Cuba were a compilation of mixed architectural styles, dominated by the Plateresque style, which gets its name from the delicate filigree workmanship of the Spanish silversmith's decorative art, *platería*. Many buildings also had Romanesque and/or Gothic elements and thereby defy any specific

architectural periodization other than Spanish Colonial. Spain's sixteenth-century furniture, although known for its simplicity of line and its sobriety, also had a particular richness in style.

During the XVI century Spanish secular and religious furniture was built with such luxurious and rich materials and decoration that it equaled the best of France, Germany, and England. Italian pieces were the only ones that could compete with and even surpass our cabinets, chests, coffers, small buffets, frames, and reliquaries adorned with ivory, mother-of-pearl and shell, with rich applications of chased silver and gilded bronze.[10]

It is significant that in 1492, as Columbus discovered Cuba, Muslim power was officially surrendered in Granada, Spain, after 800 years of rule. Although Moorish occupation had been terminated, Spain's architecture and furniture had nonetheless absorbed a number of Arab features. In describing this Mudéjar style, historian Mildred Stapley explains:

During the various waves of foreign influence—Flemish and Italian in the XVI century and French later—this one internal semi-Oriental influence never ceased to operate. Until shortly after the year 1600 the great majority of Spanish artisans were Moors, and from their Arab art Spain accepted all that was practical from the Christian point of view, the fusion being known as Mudéjar.[11]

Because most of the Spanish furniture-makers were Moors, they incorporated Moorish methods of construction and ornament, which in turn became a distinctive feature in many of Cuba's furniture forms. As one writer on the Moorish style notes,

In Spain, a Moorish tradition of carpentry skill has been handed down over the centuries. The Mudéjar artesonado *ceiling with its*

FIG. 34. TURNED WOODEN WINDOW GRILLES, KNOWN AS *REJAS* OR *BARROTES*. THE WINDOWS WERE TRADITIONALLY DRAPED INSIDE WITH LIGHT CLOTH TO ALLOW VENTILATION AND TO PROVIDE PRIVACY.

FIG. 35. THE NEOCLASSICAL PARISH CHURCH OF THE SANTÍSIMA TRINIDAD ON THE PLAZA IN THE COLONIAL CITY OF TRINIDAD WAS COMPLETED IN 1892.

geometric patterning has affected the vernacular design of paneled doors and ceilings today. The rules that were laid down by municipal authorities to govern the construction of timber roof structures incorporating the decorative ceilings are typified by those written in 1619 by Diego Lopez de Arenas, who was the municipal surveyor of Seville and specialized in carpentry. These rules referred to "la carpintería de lo blanco" (woodwork) and covered the type of structure, the dimensions of the members to be used, as well as the framework and the decorative patterns of the ceiling…. This publication appeared after the deportation of the remaining Moors, but by then the Moorish tradition of carpentry had been absorbed into the Spanish architectural tradition and had spread to Spanish colonies in the Americas. Many of the interlacing geometric patterns are directly descended from Islamic precedent.[12]

From the establishment of the first Spanish colony in Cuba until the late sixteenth century, the majority of furnishings in the New World came from Europe. It was the European imported furniture—especially Spanish—that first adorned the Cuban churches, government offices, and homes, and was subsequently used as templates for the first locally made pieces.

During the last half of the sixteenth century there were between fifty and sixty artisans including silversmiths, carpenters, and masons established in Havana. Other than the furniture itself, only a few written journals, wills, and inventories, and even fewer drawings and paintings survive as documentation of early Cuban colonial interiors and furnishings.

The furnishing of the earliest Havana homes during the sixteenth century tended to be rustic and improvised, not even attempting a rudimentary imitation of the Spanish models. As the first colonists adopted, for strictly practical reasons, the native style of housing, so they went on to copy the local furniture of plain benches and tables as there was

plenty of timber, especially palm wood.
Once the colony was well established, it
began to import furniture from Spain,
which was soon being reproduced by local
craftsmen; these pieces exhibited the Mudéjar
influence that was fashionable at the time.
They included "friars' armchairs" (sillón frailero), *massive embossed leather*
chests, many-drawered bargueño *desks, and a dais, the largest item in the family home,*
serving as a work area by day and sleeping couch by night.[13]

Most existing sixteenth- and early seventeenth-century furniture, whether island-made or imported, is ecclesiastical, and as a result, only monastic and church pieces of furniture are documented. Surviving pieces include sacristy cupboards or armoires, sacristy chests, and chairs. The earliest recorded historical mention of furniture on Cuba referred to sixteenth-century "Spanish chairs" (*taburetes*), which had leather seats and backrests with copper or brass studs to secure the leather. With the exception of the armoires, all furniture forms were simple in design, with no surface decoration. No furniture-makers' names have been discovered in journals and craftsmen never signed or branded pieces of furniture.

In order to establish the first colonial towns, virgin forests were cut. In María Luisa Lobo Montalvo's description, exotic tropical hardwoods were the first prize of the New World and important commodities in island commerce.

Around this port shipyards became established and renowned, making shipbuilding one of
the town's major economic resources. Cedar, mahogany, sabicu, and other precious timbers,
felled in the island's woods, were prodigiously used in the industry, hewn into majestic,
shapely galleons destined for the various Spanish armadas.[14]

It was in Cuba's coastal forests that the various exotic tropical hardwoods were found, especially mahogany (*Swietenia mahagoni*), which eventually became the wood of choice for furniture-makers throughout Europe, North America, and the West Indies.

The astonishing value of Cuban wood was one of the things that were discovered by
Columbus. Among the woods are the lignum vitae; the cocoa wood or cocus, which some-

FIG. 39. A BEACH, POSSIBLY THE ONE WHERE COLUMBUS LANDED ON SUNDAY, OCTOBER 28, 1492. CUBA HAS THOUSANDS OF SIMILAR BEACHES ALONG ITS COAST.

OPPOSITE:
FIG. 38. THE PATIO OF THE MONASTERY OF SAN FRANCISCO DE ASÍS, BUILT IN THE 1730S, HAS GALLERIES ON THREE LEVELS. IT WAS THE MOST ELEGANT AND FASHIONABLE STRUCTURE IN HAVANA IN ITS TIME.

FIG. 40. THE CATHEDRAL OF
HAVANA, WITH ITS IMPOSING
AND EXUBERANTLY SCROLLED
FAÇADE, WAS BUILT IN 1748
AND DESIGNATED A CATHE-
DRAL IN 1793. THE ALTERNAT-
ING CONVEX AND CONCAVE
PLANES AND SCROLLED AND
ZIGZAG FORMS MAKE THIS
CUBA'S QUINTESSENTIAL
BAROQUE BUILDING.

what resembles the lignum vitae, and is used for similar purposes, as also for pins, and tree nails, and for turnery, making excellent flutes; the lance wood, largely exported for carriage shafts, surveyors' instruments, and other uses. Mahogany is so abundant, and the quality of wood is so superior, that it has been, since its first use in London, in 1724, an important item in the exports of the Island. Belonging to the same natural order is the Cedrela odorata *of Linnaeus, and there is much used, as also in the United States, for the inside of drawers and wardrobes. It is the material of the cigar boxes.*[15]

Legend has it that the first European furniture made of West Indian mahogany was crafted in the 1600s in Spain in the Baroque style, and that the wood was taken from a dismembered Spanish galleon that had been constructed in Cuba. By the late seventeenth century, Havana had become renowned for building the best galleons in the West Indies.

R. W. Symonds writes that the "chief sources of supply of mahogany were the virgin forest of the wood which grew in the Spanish West Indian Islands of San Domingo, Cuba, Jamaica …" He goes on to describe West Indian mahogany:

…from the island of San Domingo, a Spanish possession, hence the designation of this particular mahogany as "Spanish." Thomas Sheraton in his Cabinet Dictionary *(1803) writes that: "Hispaniola, or St. Domingo, is a West Indian island and produces dying woods and mahogany of a hardish texture, but is not much in use with us." San Domingo mahogany is of a deep red color and darkens with exposure to light and air. It is extremely hard with a smooth surface, which allows it to be easily polished. Although much of this wood is plain, it is also found with a fine figure, which adds considerably to its value. Logs of San Domingo mahogany are not of such large dimensions as those obtained from the mahogany trees of Cuba…*[16]

Aside from mahogany, similar Cuban woods were used in furniture-making: ausubo (*Manilkara bidentata*), often referred to as "bulletwood"; satinwood (*Zanthoxylum flavum*); cedar (*Cedrela odorata*); sabicu (*Lysiloma sabicu*); jacaranda (*Jacaranda mimosifolia*); and campeche (*Sickingia tinctoria*). For strength in building and construction, the woods used were lignum vitae (*Guaiacum officinale*), and almique, which is also known as "acana" (*Manilkara jaimique*). When Phillip II of Spain began to build his royal residence, El Escorial, in 1563, he used Cuba's precious hardwoods for the library and monastery choir.

FIG. 41. THE SEVENTEENTH-CEN-
TURY ALTAR OF THE IGLESIA DE
SAN JUAN BATISTA IN REMEDIOS
IS CARVED OF CEDAR IN THE
CHURRIGUERESQUE STYLE AND
COVERED WITH 24-KARAT GOLD
LEAF. ABOVE IT IS A FLUTED
AND GABLED MOORISH-STYLE
MAHOGANY CEILING TYPICAL OF
EARLY CUBAN CRAFTSMANSHIP.

El Escorial was completed in 1584 and is said to be the first use of West Indian mahogany in Europe. Soon after, mahogany and other Cuban hardwoods increased in demand and rose significantly in value.

In 1514, Diego Velázquez founded the eastern city of Santiago de Cuba, which he named after the King of Spain's patron saint, St. Jago. It was Cuba's first capital and grew rapidly. The famous conquistador Hernán Cortés, Santiago's first *capitán general,* stayed in Velázquez's home before setting out to conquer Mexico in 1519. Other conquistadors resided in Santiago as well, including the colonizer of Puerto Rico, Juan Ponce de León; Francisco Pizarro, conqueror of Peru; and Don Pedro de Alvarado, founder of Guatemala.

Diego Velázquez's villa in Santiago de Cuba, which still stands today on the Plaza Céspedes, is the best extant example of a colonial Cuban settlement house. Casa de Velázquez was built in the early 1500s in the Spanish Mudéjar style that dominated Cuban architecture at the beginning of the colonial period. The architecture of Moorish Spain included the Mudéjar-style carved ceilings (*alfarjes*) and intricate latticework window screens (*celosios*) that are found throughout Cuba. Although the term Mudéjar is usually used to describe architecture, it can also refer to furniture in the Hispano-Moresque style that has surface decoration similar to that of Mudéjar architecture, or that incorporates Moorish methods of construction.

Certain universal construction methods are most associated with Spanish furniture. The way in which dovetail, mortise and tenon, or tongue and groove joints were fabricated can be an aid in the identification of Hispanic furniture, and may help in differentiating Iberian from colonial pieces—although in some periods there is no exact way of making these distinctions. Joinery changed little once the methods had been learned, but it is the special old design of classic joints, which now enables one to recognize the Hispanic touch.[17]

Inside Casa de Velázquez, the rooms are dark and cool. The furniture is plush and opulent for sixteenth- and seventeenth-century forms, and the grilled trelliswork shutters (*mosharabia*) are Mudéjar masterpieces. This early design took into consideration the island's hot, tropical climate and alternating torrential rain. The covered galleries and shuttered windows gave protection from these weather conditions, yet allowed for ventilation and light.

Gold and copper were still being mined from the mountains above Santiago de Cuba when Velázquez began the construction of his impressive residence at the corner of the city square. The year was 1516 and Governor Velázquez intended that he should be housed in a mansion befitting that of the most influential individual in the New World. Much of the raw material for his mansion was imported from Spain. However, the precious woods of Cuba proved excellent materials from which to build the framework, the flooring and the embellishments which made this one of the grandest colonial mansions ever built in the Americas.[18]

Probably the earliest, most basic, and common piece of imported furniture that was crafted in Cuba was the medieval-style six-sided chest. Constructed of six boards in box-like form, the chest was used to transport personal belongings from the mother country, for storage, as a dining surface, or as a seat. Chests built in Cuba have unusually thick boards; the native tropical hardwood was abundant and inexpensive, consequently the joiners used boards one-and one-half to two inches thick.

Many of the early chests in Cuba have a unique and curious construction joinery. The most interesting feature on the earliest Cuban colonial chests is the exposed step dovetails, more commonly referred to as "step-profiled dovetails." This intricate exposed dovetail configuration is common to Moorish workmanship from the Canary Islands.

The Moors were skilled joiners who never used iron nails or wooden pegs; instead, extremely fine joints were employed with tiny pins hidden beneath the painted or inlay fin-

One interesting feature of the earliest Cuban colonial chests is their exposed step-profiled

ishes. Their greatest contributions to the history of furniture were their use of such sophisticated techniques and above all their vocabulary of decoration ...[19]

Most of the surviving sixteenth-century and early seventeenth-century chests, often referred to as "Havana chests" (*cajas habaneras*), were constructed of cedar and often had intricate dovetailing very similar to seventeenth- and eighteenth-century Bermudian cedar chests-on-frames. Furniture scholars have long maintained that the step-profile Bermudian chest form originated in Bermuda and that its construction is unique to that island.

Without question, the most typical piece of Bermudian furniture is the chest on frame. Such chests were made in the islands from the seventeenth century into the nineteenth centuries...the purely decorative dovetails on the coffers appear to be unique to Bermudian chests on frame. It is generally accepted that individual cabinetmakers might have used their dovetail design as their signature, but no pattern has been linked to a specific maker.[20]

The step-profiled dovetail for which Bermuda cedar chests are noted can be proven to have been inspired by Hispanic-Moorish craftsmanship and was probably brought to Bermuda by sea trade from the Spanish islands. In fact, it was the Spanish sea captain Juan de Bermúdez who discovered Bermuda in the first decade of the sixteenth century. The earliest written record of Bermuda is a 1511 Spanish map depicting the island of "Bermudas"; in 1515 the Spanish explorer Fernández de Oviedo sailed to the island and attributed its discovery to his countryman Juan de Bermúdez, possibly as early as 1503.

The Spanish called Bermuda the "Island of Devils," for many of their ships foundered on the extensive reefs that surround the more than three hundred and sixty-five islands and islets that make up the archipelago. The accounts of ship-wrecked sailors who managed to build new boats and sail away from Bermuda gave the lie to the idea that devils inhabited the islands, but the myth continued until a permanent English colony was established in 1612, and it may be in part responsible for today's myths about the Bermuda Triangle.[21]

Examples of colonial Spanish cedar chests throughout Mexico and the greater Spanish Antilles, especially Cuba, date a hundred years before any documented cedar chests from Bermuda. As a result, scholars have speculated that what has been known as the Bermuda chest had Cuban and Mudéjar-inspired origins.

OPPOSITE:
FIG. 43. A PAIR OF EARLY EIGHTEENTH-CENTURY CUBAN-MADE ARMCHAIRS WITH QUEEN ANNE-STYLE YOKED CRESTRAILS AND VASIFORM SPLAT CENTERS, ALONG WITH A PARTICULARLY FINE COLONIAL CONSOLE TABLE IN THE ENGLISH STYLE

FIG. 44. DETAIL OF THE EARLY EIGHTEENTH-CENTURY CUBAN COLONIAL CONSOLE TABLE PICTURED OPPOSITE, SHOWING ONE OF THE WONDERFULLY CARVED FACES (POSSIBLY PORTRAITS OF THE FIRST OWNER WHO COMMISSIONED THE PIECE) ON THE LEGS

OVERLEAF:
FIG. 45. CUBAN BAROQUE FURNITURE FROM THE LATE SEVENTEENTH AND EARLY EIGHTEENTH CENTURIES. THE DESIGNS OF THE CHAIRS ARE SPANISH-INFLUENCED AND THE DESK IS FRENCH- AND ENGLISH-INFLUENCED.

One of Bermuda's seventeenth-century governors owned a chest that historically was thought to have originated in Bermuda.

Cedar furniture was made in Spain and the Spanish Colonies. Seventeenth-century Bermudians acquired some Spanish Colonial furniture in the West Indies (bought, bartered, or "borrowed"). The 1671 inventory of Colonel William Sayle includes a Spanish cedar chest. [22]

In Bryden Hyde's discussion on the origin of Bermudian chest construction, he considers the Moorish-Spanish influences:

But none of the English or American chest-on-frames closely resembles Bermudian ones and we must turn to Spain and her colonies for the origin of the Bermudian form. The chief point of interest is the elaborate dovetailing usually found on Bermudian and Spanish colonial ones. For it is this writer's theory that the elaborate dovetailing was developed in Spain from Moorish Mudéjar chests. [23]

There are other examples of colonial cedar chests with step-profile dovetailing that have appeared on other Caribbean islands, in Mesoamerica, and in South America that have documented provenance from the Spanish Antilles, specifically Cuba. In Ernesto Cordet's discussion on early Cuban furniture he says:

Certain pieces of furniture, regarded in the twentieth century as primitive—such as Havana chests with step-profiled dovetails, which rely for their effect on plain joinery combined with handsome iron fittings—were highly esteemed at the time and were often exported to South America. [24]

One of the most common procedures for determining the origin of a piece of furniture is wood analysis or microanalysis. Therefore, in the case of Havana and/or Bermuda chests, wood identification can determine whether the wood was native to Bermuda or Cuba. The cedar indigenous to Bermuda is actually a juniper (*Juniperus bermudiana*), known also as Eastern red cedar and pencil cedar. The cedar grown in Cuba is South American cedar (*Cedrela odorata*), known on the islands as Spanish cedar and cigar-box

FIG. 46. ALTHOUGH UNMIS-
TAKABLY INFLUENCED BY
ENGLISH AND FRENCH
ROCOCO FURNITURE,
CUBAN-MADE PIECES OF
THE EIGHTEENTH CENTURY
WERE HEAVIER AND MORE
BOLDLY PROPORTIONED
THAN EITHER, WITH EXAG-
GERATED CARVING. THE
DEEP CARVING REPLACED
THE HIGHLY ORNAMENTED
ORMOLU AND/OR GILT-
BRONZE MOUNTS POPULAR
ON EUROPEAN FURNITURE.

cedar. Early chests originally thought to have been Bermudian have proven, through wood analysis, to be made of Spanish cedar and therefore must have originated in Cuba.

Although scholars have for years accepted as axiomatic the dictum that step-profile dovetailing inevitably implies Bermuda craftsmanship, this is no longer the case. It is quite evident that the decorative dovetailing workmanship is in fact Hispanic-Moorish and first arrived in Cuba in the sixteenth century.

Spanish chests were usually constructed of dovetailed planks, with later dovetailing displayed as a decorative feature. Feduchi showed a regional Mudéjar box which illustrates that decorative dovetailing was done as early as the 1500s. Eighteenth-century dovetails were often cut in zigzags, stairsteps, and curves—so characteristic of Hispanic chests that those of Spain can seldom be distinguished from those of Mexico.[25]

A number of similar chests have been discovered in the Canary Islands, where the form is referred to as a "Canary Island chest" and the step-profile dovetail is referred to as a *diente de perro* (hound's-tooth) joint. Local history has it that these chests were first used on ships that sailed between the Canaries and Cuba. Exploration and trading patterns meant that many cedar chests found their way to Bermuda. These early Cuban cedar chests were surely used as templates for what later became, and is commonly referred to as, the Bermuda chest-on-frame. It is now safe to say that what was once thought to be an expression of form originating in Bermuda is in fact an example of Mudéjar-influenced Spanish and Cuban craftsmanship.

Another expression of form that was popular during this early colonial era was the useful and decorative Spanish imported form: the *vargueño*. *Vargueño* is a nineteenth-century term for a writing desk, which replaced the original name, *escritorio*. Considered Spain's most characteristic, distinctive, and finest cabinet type, the *vargueño* consists of upper and lower portions; the upper part is a box or chest fitted out with shelves, small drawers for valuables, and compartments with doors for documents. The drop front, which falls forward and conceals all the drawers and compartments, serves as a writing surface. The top part rests on a trestle stand or chest, in a style that has changed over the years according to fashion.

During the fifteenth century in Spain, small cabinets, beautifully wrought and inlaid, were set upon tables. In the sixteenth century the cabinet began to be attached to the table. Soon the table developed into an elaborately carved stand for the ever-growing cabinet which took unto itself drawers, compartments, and folding tops. This combined piece—which might suggest to us a heavy, richly carved highboy—developed into the magnificent ensemble called a vargueño.[26]

The form is unquestionably Spanish in origin, although it was erroneously formerly thought to have been invented in Vargas, a village near Toledo. It is Hispanic-Arab in design and execution.

Not much that is certain is known about the famous vargueños *that according to tradition were created in Vargas, a town in the province of Toledo. Certainly in Vargas there is no record of any carpenter's shop or workshop for fashioning the furniture or any other. Possibly the name* vargueño *came from a workshop in Toledo in the XVI century, whose owner, a master carver and cabinetmaker, was named Vargas.*[27]

Instead, as the interiors of the first Spanish *vargueños* were intricately inlaid in geometrical patterns of bone or ivory, the expression of form was likely of Moorish origin. The tour de force of the Spanish cabinetmakers' art, most of the *vargueño* writing desks on the island were imported, as it was not a form commonly copied in Cuba. In the rare instance that it was copied, the Cuban *vargueño* was far less sophisticated in craftsmanship and composition. There are also examples of *papeleras,* which is essentially the same form but without the hinged drop front. Early inventories found on Jamaica before the English expelled the Spaniards, documented *vargueños* that belonged to wealthy Spaniards; these *vargueños* were inlaid with ivory and tortoise shell and therefore must have been imported from Spain.

More commonly found are island-made chairs and armoires, which follow Spanish models closely. As previously mentioned, one of the first records of Cuban furniture is the *taburete,* or side chair, made of Cuban cedar or hardwood with a leather back panel stretched between the upright supports and a leather seat panel stretched between the seat rails. Both back and seat panels are securely attached with decorative copper or brass nails to the frame. These chairs are a basic Spanish Renaissance form that is simply designed with plain, undecorated surfaces.

FIG. 49. ONE OF THE MANY
BEACHES ON THE MORE THAN
1,600 CAYS (LOW CORAL
BANKS) THAT SURROUND CUBA

FIG. 50. A COLLECTION OF
EIGHTEENTH- AND NINE-
TEENTH-CENTURY HAND-
CARVED AND POLYCHROMED
SPANISH COLONIAL ECCLESI-
ASTICAL FIGURES ATOP AN
ISLAND-MADE ANTIQUE
MAHOGANY ARMOIRE

The *sillón de caderas* can be described as a Spanish hip-joint chair. The pre-Renaissance form, probably of Moorish origin, found its way to Europe during Roman times. This earliest type of Spanish chair is of the curule type—a folding, X-form chair—made of wood or metal. All the examples of this form found in Cuba were either of Spanish origin or nineteenth-century copies. That is not to say that the curule form was not copied before the nineteenth century by island craftsmen, but very few remain intact. The Campeche chair crafted in Cuba in the eighteenth century incorporated the curule base form, and is discussed in Chapter III.

The earliest Cuban armchairs, *sillones fraileros* ("friars' chairs"), were also simple, austere, and rectangular. They were made of cedar or island hardwood with plain quadrangle supports and mortise and tenon construction. Later in the sixteenth century and into the seventeenth century, a broad front stretcher with S-scrolls or volute carving assumed a decorative character and became a most distinguishing feature. As in the *taburetes,* leather was attached to the seat and back frames by large decorative nails. The form, derived from sixteenth-century Spanish examples, was inspired by the folding chair (*sillón de caderas*) and continued to be made in Cuba throughout the nineteenth century with little stylistic variation. These chairs came to be identified with the island's colonial way of life.

Plain benches (*bancos*) were used everywhere from the cathedral sacristy to the humblest of Cuban kitchens. Most of the early benches are demountable, with an undecorated, hinged back that enabled it to be folded down on the seat. The legs could either be taken off the frame or folded under the seat, as well. Late in the century and during the seventeenth century, the backs became more decorative and were carved in the typical Cuban Plateresque or Baroque manner.

Armoires or wardrobes (*roperos*) were rarely seen outside churches and were generally plain with simple construction and usually made from island cedar. Most examples are designed with a frame and panel, mortise and tenon construction. In rare instances, armoire doors have Mudéjar geometric designs and, in some cases, names of the owner or family are carved on the doors or sides of the piece.

austere forms made of cedar or island hardwood with leather seats attached by large nails

Chapter II   COLONIZATION: THE SEVENTEENTH CENTURY

FIG. 51. ORNAMENTAL DESIGNS IN THE CROSS-BEAMS, OR *TIRANTES*, WHICH DISTINGUISH THE MUDÉJAR-INSPIRED *ALFARJE* CEILINGS, BECAME MORE OPEN AND LIGHTER IN CONSTRUCTION THAN THOSE OF THE PREVIOUS CENTURY.

By the seventeenth century, Philip II of Spain had declared Cuba to be the "threshold and key to the New World." The Viceroyalty of Spanish America included the Antilles, present-day Venezuela, Mexico, Central America, Florida, a large part of the southwestern United States, and the Philippines. Trade with the Philippines was established in the 1560s, linking Spain and China. The Manila Galleon brought Asian imports such as porcelain, lacquer work, sumptuous silks, and jewels to Acapulco, where they were transported overland to Veracruz on Mexico's east, and then on to Spain by way of Cuba. The reverse trade route, the Flota Indiana (Indies Fleet), which traveled from Spain to Cuba, and then on to South America and Mexico, brought European luxury goods to Cuba and New Spain for consumption by the Spanish and Creole (Spanish-born in the Americas) aristocracy. The arrival of the Flota Indiana in the port of Veracruz meant an influx of fine embossed and gilded cordovan leather for upholstering the furniture and walls of the most important spaces in private homes; Spanish rugs destined for luxurious drawing rooms and bedchambers; gold and silver thread that added a touch of elegance to intricately embroidered imported fabrics; lace from Flanders or Lorraine for trimming garments and household linens; Flemish paintings of landscapes and mythological themes; Spanish and Italian escritoires made of fine woods; fancy German tablecloths; Venetian glass; tortoise-shell writing desks from Italy; small bottles from Castile; glass picture frames from Flanders; upholstery and drapery materials from Brussels; jet ornaments from Santiago de Compostela; and so forth. Any person of means was expected to flaunt his or her wealth by forming an ample collection of such objects, always keeping them in plain sight.[28]

Many of the luxury goods from both the Orient and Europe (particularly Italy and Flanders) remained in Cuba and influenced the fashion and customs of Cuban nobility through the 1600s. During these colonial years, Cuba's economy depended on supplying the Spanish fleet both by trading in European and New World goods and exporting the island's natural resources.

Although the Spanish thalassocracy had been broken in 1588 by the English defeat of the Spanish Armada, most attempts by European powers to break Spanish territorial power in the West Indies and their trade monopoly had failed. However, England, France, Holland, and Denmark had begun colonizing the West Indies. In 1642, Acapulco was invaded by the Dutch, who also seized the islands of Curaçao, St. Martin, St. Eustatius, and Saba by 1650. England and France raided the Spanish Antilles and set up their own island colonies. In 1655, England had claimed the Spanish island of Jamaica and had founded settlements in Barbados, St. Christopher, Nevis, Antigua, and Montserrat; and France was well on its way to establishing settlements on Martinique and Guadeloupe. Meanwhile, Denmark was establishing its West Indian colony in the Virgin Islands. All of these settlements and the resulting inter-island shipping trade brought about further stylistic influences in seventeenth-century Cuban taste and fashion.

FIG. 52. PATIOS WERE INCOR-
PORATED INTO THE COLONIAL
ARCHITECTURE OF THE TROPI-
CAL SPANISH ANTILLES TO
FACILITATE AIRFLOW THROUGH
URBAN MANSIONS THAT WERE
BUILT CLOSE TO ONE
ANOTHER.

Spain's Plateresque style had reached Cuba by 1600 and was applied to many of the earliest buildings on the island. Havana had grown into a city and was made Cuba's capital in 1607; by 1674 the city walls were completed.

The city of Havana was formally the city of San Cristóbal de la Habana, San Cristobal of the Plain, and is still referred to always in Spanish as "La Habana." The "b" in Habana came into usage in the mid-eighteenth century, the word being always previously spelled with a "v," like most Spanish bs till then.[29]

Havana's oldest extant church, Espiritu Santo (Holy Ghost), was built in 1632 by freed African slaves. Although it was dedicated in 1638, the façade was not completed until 1674. The Convento de Santa Clara (Convent of Santa Clara) was founded in 1644 by Sister Catalina de Mendoza from Cartagena de Indias, and offered refuge to the poorer girls of Havana. The convent has the finest extant example of a Mudéjar interior with its Moorish trussed ceilings that featured a variety of carvings. Other seventeenth-century structures (including city residences) included fine Mudéjar carpentry, which was profusely decorated in intricate geometric patterns. By the mid-seventeenth century, the first evidence of an embellished Plateresque style—or what was to develop into the Cuban Baroque style—became fashionable. Seventeenth-century colonial houses, although not as large as those that would be built in the 1700s, were considered quite large, and incorporated many Spanish designs that combined modifications for the tropical climate, such as high ceilings, verandas, heavily shuttered windows and doors, and patios.

The Mudéjar patio plan, the nucleus of the colonial Cuban house, probably came into use in the early seventeenth century as settlers adopted increasingly sophisticated designs and built more permanent structures. The enclosed open-air patio was directly derived from a feature of medieval Arabic architecture, the private inner court where women were cloistered and most domestic activities occurred. Its introduction in Cuba was important in that it signaled the first transition from a primitive one-room plan to a layout that assigned specific uses to specific spaces. The patio was also a necessary means of ventilation for contiguous houses that shared bearing walls.

The fundamental concept of the patio plan depended on a hierarchy of rooms (with graduated size and ceiling heights) moving from public and formal to casual and private. At the front was the best sala, *generally a showplace for furniture, and one or two* aposentos,

FIG. 53. TYPICAL OF THE ANI-
MAL MILLS USED TO CRUSH
SUGAR CANE IN CUBA, THIS
EXAMPLE WAS POWERED BY AN
OX TETHERED TO THE OVER-
HEAD BOOM. THE ANIMAL WAS
WALKED AROUND THE MILL,
TURNING THE ROLLERS THAT
CRUSHED THE CANE.

or bedrooms, with a smaller saleta *and flanking* recámaras *(less important bedrooms) located directly to the rear.*[30]

Most of the urban mansions had enclosed, arcaded courtyards and patios. With the arrival of this more ornate architectural period, furniture incorporated more decorative forms and motifs as well.

The austerity of Cuban furniture during the first half of the seventeenth century followed the contemporaneous Spanish style and differed little stylistically from that of the previous century. But by the middle of the 1600s, furniture had become more decorative. Surfaces on chair stretchers, chest rails, armoire doors, or table aprons were carved with decorative motifs. The more elaborate furniture styles therefore followed the development of the elaborate Cuban architectural style, as the craftsmen who were making the furniture were the same housewrights and woodworkers who were constructing the island's buildings and their interiors.

The design and decoration of the few extant wardrobes is similar to the workmanship found on doors and windows. These pieces, together with documented payments to carpenters, indicate that the Cuban craftsmen who made furniture during this period were the same tradesmen responsible for doors, windows and general home carpentry.[31]

The appearance of Plateresque decoration on domestic furniture was influenced by its use on ecclesiastical forms, including altarpieces, pulpits, pews, sacristy chests of drawers, and armoires.

It was during the seventeenth century that another change—in fact a profound social revolution—began: the cultivation of sugar cane on a large scale. Whereas the previous century had been one of discovery and conquest in the Caribbean, the seventeenth century's introduction of vast sugar plantations worked by slaves represented an enormous accession of wealth and power. The Spaniards had been growing sugar in Hispaniola in small quantities for a century, but they had never fully exploited its possibilities. Their Catholic rivals, the Portuguese, had extensive and better organized sugar plantations in Brazil. The Dutch, who had learned the secrets of sugar cultivation in the Brazilian state of Pernombuco, were economically motivated to share their knowledge and encouraged the production of sugar throughout the West Indies because they were the Caribbean merchants and traders.

to Europe by Crusaders. It was first used medicinally, and was regarded as a rare luxury.

In the years between 1604 and 1640 English, Dutch, and French colonists—cooperating with each other against the Spaniards—selected their first colonizing sites in the Caribbean. This was the great age of Dutch commercial expansion, and the Hollanders turned the Caribbean almost into a Dutch lake.[32]

Hence it was the Dutch who first brought the sugar industry to Spain's rivals and their colonies in the West Indies.

Sugar was originally cultivated in India, brought to the Middle East by Arabs, and introduced into Europe with the return of the Crusaders. It was first used medicinally and was regarded as a rare luxury. The Spaniards first cultivated it in the Canary, Madeira, and Azores Islands, and Columbus brought it to the West Indies.

FIG. 54. A CUBAN SUGAR CANE FIELD IN THE VALLEY OF THE SUGAR MILLS (VALLE DE LOS INGENIOS). SUGAR CANE, WHICH WAS INTRODUCED TO CUBA BY THE SPANISH, BECAME THE ISLAND'S PRE-DOMINANT CROP BY THE EIGHTEENTH CENTURY.

Sugar cane seems to have been already brought, incidentally, in a very modest way, to the Caribbean: perhaps even by Columbus, on his second voyage, in 1493. A colonist named Aguilón was apparently growing cane in Concepción de la Vega, Santo Domingo, as early as 1505; he is said by Las Casas to have ground the cane with 'certain wooden instruments which obtained juice.' No doubt these were brought from Madeira or the Canary Islands.[33]

By the mid-seventeenth century, sugar was the most important product on the French and English islands; however, on the Spanish islands it remained only one of many exported products and not of supreme importance until the eighteenth century. Europe's demand for sugar coincided with the popularity of tea and coffee. The bride of Charles II of England, Catherine of Braganza (daughter of the king of Portugal), was the first to introduce a taste for tea to England. The first London coffee houses opened in the early 1650s, teahouses opened a decade later, and chocolate was introduced soon thereafter. Coffee and tea rivaled each other and both competed with cocoa, but all required a taste for sugar. Before the 1600s West Indian planters were producing low-grade sugar called *muscovado*, but soon after they learned how to refine it into white sugar. After seizing Jamaica from the Spanish in 1655, the English turned their attention to sugar and by the 1670s they were producing over 750 tons of sugar annually on the island of Jamaica.

In addition to building the sugar plantations, the seventeenth-century sugar planters and merchants of the Caribbean created one of the cruelest and harshest systems of servitude in history. As the Caribbean's most important source of wealth, agriculture—particularly sugar

FIG. 56. THIS DESK IN THE
LUIS LAS CASAS STYLE, WITH
ENGLISH INFLUENCES AND
FRENCH ROCOCO MOTIFS,
IS UNMISTAKABLY CUBAN
BECAUSE OF ITS MAHOGANY
SECONDARY WOOD CONSTRUC-
TION AND ITS BOLD PROPOR-
TIONS. THE CRUCIFIX AND
MAHOGANY CASE ARE ALSO
EIGHTEENTH-CENTURY.
CATHOLICISM WAS AN IMPOR-
TANT PART OF COLONIAL LIFE
FOR CUBANS, ESPECIALLY
THOSE OF SPANISH DESCENT.

OPPOSITE:
FIG. 55. EIGHTEENTH-CEN-
TURY FURNITURE IN THE LUIS
LAS CASAS STYLE IN THE DIN-
ING ROOM OF THE CASA DE
DIEGO VELÁZQUEZ. THIS
STYLE, WHICH IS PARTICULAR
TO CUBA, COMBINES ENGLISH
AND FRENCH ELEMENTS.

OVERLEAF:
FIG. 57. AN EARLY COLONIAL
BEDROOM, OR APOSENTO,
THAT ADJOINS A SITTING
ROOM, OR SALETA. THE
SEVENTEENTH-CENTURY
BED HAS TURNED POSTS
SIMILAR TO THOSE OF
PORTUGESE BEDS OF THE
PERIOD.

production—became inseparable from the exploitation of African slave labor. Slavery on the islands has been described as a "monstrous aberration" politically as well as morally. The origins of African slavery in the West Indies, and especially in the Spanish Antilles, go hand in hand with the success of sugar agriculture.

The origin and character of African West Indian enslavement is a sensitive and provocative tropic. Its relevance to Cuban colonial furniture is important in the sense that in many documented cases—and assuredly many more undocumented cases—colonial furniture was crafted by enslaved or descendants of enslaved African-West Indian woodworkers. The success of Cuba's colonial agriculture systems of sugar, coffee, and tobacco depended on slave labor; enslaved African workers, who were referred to as "black gold" and "black ivory," were the indispensable basis of the island's plantation economy. From the seventeenth to the nineteenth centuries, hundreds of thousands of African men, women, and children were imported to and sold in Cuba.

Slavery in Cuba began as early as 1517 when the Emperor Charles V, who succeeded King Ferdinand as the king of Spain, granted concessions or licenses to supply African slaves to the West Indies. Called an *asiento* (a monopoly contract), this tax-free concession became a most coveted license. The rights of the *asiento* allowed for the importation of four thousand African slaves annually to Spanish America. One of the earliest instances of Africans being brought to Cuba is described in Hugh Thomas's scholarly book, *The Slave Trade*:

> *A few of the first generation of black slaves in the Americas played a part in the next wave of conquests. Diego Velázquez had had a few African slaves with him in 1511–12 in his occupation of Cuba, an island which would eventually develop a black culture more profound than anywhere else in the Spanish empire.*[34]

By the mid-seventeenth century, there were between fifteen thousand and twenty thousand enslaved Africans in the Spanish Antilles. Due to strict Spanish laws that limited the number of African slaves, the Spanish island planters relied on Dutch, English and French smugglers for additional slaves, thereby denying the Spanish Crown the required taxes.

FIG. 58. BEAUTIFUL IRONWORK, SUCH AS THIS VICTORIAN CAST-IRON GARDEN BENCH, IS FOUND THROUGHOUT CUBA.

FIG. 59. ONE OF MANY DECORATIVE WROUGHT-IRON WHEEL-GUARDS THAT WERE PLACED ON EITHER SIDE OF WIDE ENTRANCES FROM THE STREET TO PROTECT THE CORNERS FROM SCRAPING BY CARRIAGE WHEEL-HUBS.

The Spanish took no direct part in the African end of the trade at this period, but their American possessions were the ultimate destination of perhaps one-fifth of all slaves that reached the new world in the late seventeenth century. Fearing Protestant pollution of their Catholic realm and breach of their monopolies of gold and silver, the Spanish forbade almost all trade between their settlers in America and other Europeans. Spanish settlers got their slaves by welcoming foreign ships to their ports in violation of royal commands, by going to Jamaica, Curaçao, and so on to trade, and by taking advantage of a major legal concession called the asiento, *in which a Spanish or foreign merchant combine received, in return for a large advance on the duties it would owe and other contributions to the Spanish crown, a near monopoly of the legal delivery of slaves to Spanish American ports.*[35]

In an effort to regain slave revenue, the Spanish crown in 1651 allowed its merchants to trade in African slaves in order to supply the islands with what was considered the necessary labor force. Throughout the century, the Spanish government continued to award *asientos* and tens of thousands of slaves were imported to the islands. The slave trade represented one of the largest commercial enterprises during the colonial era. Slave traders made fortunes, as was explained in 1685: "Everyone knows that the slave trade is the source of the wealth which the Spaniards wring out of the West Indies, and that whoever knows how to furnish them slaves, will share their wealth."[36] Cuban slave revolts broke out as early as 1729 and 1731 in the copper mines of Santiago but the *asientos* were ruled lawful and the supply of African slaves to the Spanish colonies continued for another 150 years. In 1820 the Spanish government signed a treaty with England and pledged abolition, but it wasn't until 1886 that slavery was truly abolished in Cuba.

Colonial Cuban cabinetmakers comprised a combination of trained joiners and cabinetmakers who had immigrated to Cuba not only from Spain, the Canary Islands, and possibly other West Indian Islands, but also from the importation of African enslaved woodworkers who learned furniture-making in some cases by apprenticing with island cabinetmakers. "[B]ut, also most of the non-European craftspeople were of African descent, since whites nursed a lamentable contempt for any trade they considered demeaning."[37]

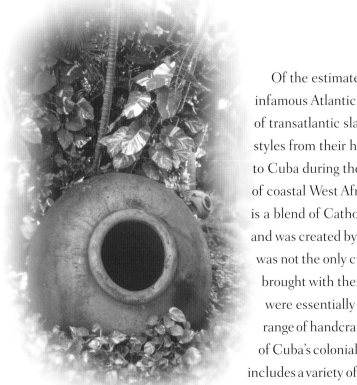

Of the estimated 100,000 enslaved Africans who crossed the infamous Atlantic "middle passage" to Cuba during three centuries of transatlantic slavery, many "brought with them techniques and styles from their homelands."[38] Most of the African slaves imported to Cuba during the colonial period were from the middle stretches of coastal West Africa. *Santería*, a religion practiced in Cuba today, is a blend of Catholicism and the polytheistic beliefs of West Africa, and was created by enslaved Africans and their descendants. Religion was not the only cultural aspect that was imported. The Africans brought with them many variations of their native enterprises. "All were essentially agricultural but they possessed also a considerable range of handcraft industries and wide trade connections."[39] Much of Cuba's colonial furniture represents a vernacular style that includes a variety of traditional Hispanic-Moorish, African, and European construction techniques and a mélange of decorative motifs.

As tobacco and sugar cultivation expanded and became more profitable, colonists built larger houses and furnished them with luxury items such as silver, more elaborate furniture, porcelain, glass, wall hangings, and table linen. As the amount of living space increased, the design of the townhouses remained similar to those built earlier in the century. Two-story—and in rare instances three-story—houses were built around a patio or central courtyard with tile-roofed timber balconies and arcades on the ground and upper floors. Unlike the French, Dutch, Danish, and English island colonies, the Spaniards' residences, known as "great houses," were built in the urban centers.

Many of the land-owning plantocracy lived in Spain, but those who lived in Cuba preferred to reside in the city or town nearest their plantations. Consequently, the largest and most luxurious residences were situated away from the sugar plantations (*ingenios*) and coffee plantations (*cafetales*).

> *The towns of the Spanish islands are well planned, dignified, and often architecturally distinguished, unlike the haphazard and often mean collections of buildings in the British colonies; but Cuba and Puerto Rico have nothing comparable with the Georgian 'great houses' of Jamaica and Barbados.*[40]

the result that the most luxurious residences were urban mansions rather than country houses.

Although palatial residences were built in urban areas, less elaborate country estates or plantation homes were concurrently constructed and also contained many fashionable furnishings. However, the most luxurious furniture was found in the urban mansions that were the plantation owner's showplace.

As previously mentioned, furniture from the latter part of the seventeenth century had become more decorative than it had been earlier, and form had become more important than function. Carving and turning were increasingly embellished. Definitive turning had become fashionable, particularly in chair and table legs and bedposts. There are Cuban examples of elaborately turned reel-and-bobbin bedposts that are very similar to Portuguese (and the other Iberian-culture) posts from the same period. Curvilinear, as opposed to rectilinear, geometric carving and intricate turning gave Cuban furniture its colonial Plateresque styling. By the end of the 1600s, the Plateresque style had become even more embellished and elaborate than before; and the arrival of the Spanish Baroque was evident not only in architecture but furniture as well.

Furniture such as chests with domed, shaped lids and geometric chip carving (*montañesa*) and large paneled wardrobes began to be made of island mahogany. The cedar *cajas habaneras* (Havana chests), Cuban-made chairs and benches were exported to other Spanish colonies in the Americas from Havana. The arrival of imported, ornate *vargueños* made in Spain but crafted with Cuban ebony and mahogany and Caribbean tortoiseshell influenced Cuban craftsmen, who began using thinner wood and applied carved-wood decorations rather than actually carving the wood itself.

Although leather was preferred for seating furniture, caning and woven rattan made their first appearance in Cuba in the late 1600s. These techniques originated in China, where they were fashionable in the late 1500s, and were introduced to Europe by Portuguese and Dutch traders coming from the Orient. The Portuguese princess Catherine de Braganza, wife of Charles II of England, introduced the Baroque fashion of caned furniture to her husband's country in the mid-seventeenth century. In France, caning gained popularity in the second and third quarters of the eighteenth century and again during the early nineteenth-century Empire period. Cuban chair-makers who imitated the European style therefore incorporated caning into their work in the same manner.

Chapter III AN ERA OF PROSPERITY: THE EIGHTEENTH CENTURY

The eighteenth century was ushered in by the death of Charles II of Spain on November 1, 1700. Before his death, Charles had declared that Philip, duke of Anjou, a grandson of the Sun King Louis XIV of France, would inherit the Spanish throne as Philip V. However, the idea that the Catholic nations of France and Spain might be unified was a threat to Europe's other two great powers, Protestant Holland and England. Holland and England wanted to curtail Louis XIV's ambitions, and the West Indies proved to be an ideal battlefield. The War of the Spanish Succession began in 1702 and lasted eleven years, but the Anglo-French rivalry that began in 1700 lasted more than a century.

The establishment of the French Bourbon dynasty on the Spanish throne produced a monumental change in shipping and trade between Europe and New Spain, and it benefited Cuba with a new access to European goods. The French were particularly eager to buy Cuban tobacco, and were willing to trade any French product to procure it. In addition to the French influence in Cuba, there was also that of the British. When the French were unable to supply the demand of the Spanish Antilles for enslaved laborers, the British stepped in.

The consequence was that, when the Treaty of Utrecht came to be drawn up in 1713, to conclude the War of the Spanish Succession, the British were able to insist on taking over asiento.

Though a Bourbon ruled in Madrid, British ships would carry Africans to the Americas to work in the haciendas, the palaces, the mines, and the tobacco and sugar farms of the empire.[41]

The treaty presented opportunities for both countries in that not only did the *asiento* grant Britain permission to import enslaved Africans to Cuba for thirty years, but the right to import British products to the island, as well. "The doors of New Spain opened to French, Dutch and especially English traders, and thus furniture from England became fashionable."[42] French and English trading links to Cuba were well established by the second decade of the eighteenth century, and Cuban fashions, especially furniture, became increasingly influenced.

The restrained traditional furniture of the seventeenth century underwent a dramatic change with the importation of other European styles to both Spain and Cuba.

Different styles coexisted and were occasionally combined in single pieces of Cuban furniture. Other pieces were influenced by the English Queen Anne and Chippendale styles or reflected French designs or the Provençal style. Dutch influence is also discernible, but the persistence of Spanish decorative traditions is most obvious. These stylistic trends were partly the result of trade with Europe but may also have been due to immigrant tradesmen.[43]

In 1700, tobacco (*Nicotiane tabac*) was the island's main export; Cuba filled European noses with snuff. By 1717, the Spanish Crown had built its first factory on the island and monopolized and controlled the tobacco trade, which enraged the Cuban tobacco farmers (*vegneros*) to the point of rebellion. This was the first armed insurrection in Cuba against the Spanish Crown.

Since its initial discovery, tobacco has been an inextricable part of Cuban life. Indigenous to the island and smoked by the Amerindians, tobacco plants were brought back to Spain in the sixteenth century. First thought to be only good for medicinal purposes, by the seventeenth century tobacco had gained acceptance and was well on its way to becoming one of the New World's most desired luxuries. Cuban tobacco was not only filling the noses of European aristocrats but of the nobility of the New World as well.

A practice that became popular among ladies during the seventeenth century was the use of snuff. This odd ritual continued into the next century and was considered elegant in elite circles of colonial society. The snuffbox was de rigueur for both men and women as a stylish way to carry a day's ration of tobacco. In the salón de estrado, *it was common to see ladies opening their little boxes and taking a pinch of snuff that they inhaled. When the inevitable sneeze seemed imminent, they would politely cover their noses with ornately embroidered handkerchiefs trimmed with imported lace from Flanders or Lorraine.*[44]

By the turn of the eighteenth century, Havana had become the third largest city in the New World (after Mexico City and Lima), and part of that growth was due to the success of the tobacco trade. Tobacco was Cuba's most profitable agricultural crop until sugar gained the lead later in the eighteenth century, whereupon most colonial planters discontinued tobacco farming and turned to sugar cane.

During the seventeenth century Havana gradually became the capital of the production and dispatch of tobacco, not only toward Spain but the whole empire: Mexico, Costa Rica, and the countries of the Pacific shore. "Nothing is more important than tobacco," they used to say in Cuba.[45]

By the mid-eighteenth century Cuba was exporting over 800 tons of tobacco a year to the mother
country and the manufacture of cigars had begun.
Throughout the 1800s, tobacco was mostly con-
sumed in pipes and inhaled as snuff, but by the
end of the century the world embraced the habit
of smoking cigars and Cuba's annual production of
tobacco had reached the 3,000-ton mark. As the
plant is best grown on a small scale, the colonial
tobacco planters owned numerous smaller estates
and tracts of land. Considered a cottage industry, tobacco
exportation was in fact controlled by a few Spanish and
Creole landowners and merchants. Not all of these rich landowners
and merchants lived in Havana. By the second half of the eighteenth century, Cuban
tobacco and sugar industries all over the island began to flourish and smaller provincial colonial cities such as Trinidad, Santiago, Santa Clara, and Camagüey
boasted of great wealth. The plantation owners, merchants, and shippers
continued to increase agricultural productivity in the rural areas and
expanded foreign trade; this, in turn, brought increased riches and an
aristocracy that demanded the latest fashion in homes and furnishings.
The early eighteenth-century provincial homes were one story and later
developed into two-story houses. These houses, although smaller than
those in Havana, were elegant and had deep eaves and arcades, which
provided shade, as well as terracotta roof tiles. Much of the extant
eighteenth-century furniture that has been found outside of Havana
is as sophisticated as furniture from the capital.

*This kind of luxury was the norm on the periphery of Havana,
where planters and other grandees had splendid manors, not only in
the villages but also on sugar plantations, coffee estates, and other
properties.*[46]

LA HABANA.

General bird's eye view of Havana.

Vue de la Havane à vol d'oiseau.

Foreign influence is particularly evident in the prevailing baroque curvilinear designs; chairs and tables were more profusely carved and with increasingly more curved and undulating lines.

Cuba, as a major commercial center, continued to import objects from the Old World, and other New World Spanish possessions. Furniture and porcelain from Europe, silver objects from present-day Columbia and Peru, jewelry and decorative arts from Mexico flowed into Havana and other port cities to the Cuban provinces.[47]

Most decorative arts scholars will agree that French architecture, furniture styles, and interior decoration dominated European design until shortly after the mid-nineteenth century and the Baroque style was no exception. The Baroque style had developed in France

during the reign of Louis XIV (1643–1715), and it influenced Cuban fashion both directly and indirectly through Spain. The emergence of the Cuban Baroque style both in architecture and furniture had its roots in the Spanish Plateresque style, which, in turn, had also been influenced by French art.

As in any vernacular architectural style, Cuban construction was a gradual process of assimilation and adaptation. By the eighteenth century, however, the amalgamation of cultural traditions, accommodations to the tropical climate of the Caribbean, and European fashion trends had brought about a unique Cuban Baroque architectural style. The eighteenth-century Cuban Baroque style, with its lavishly ornamented façades, was the expression of artisans who had adapted their visions to island conditions. This heavily ornamented style reached its zenith during the late eighteenth century, both in Havana and the smaller cities, whether it was in a single-story provincial house with finely turned wood window grilles (*rejas*), or in the palaces built for the Creole aristocracy in Havana.

When all Cuban governmental administrative offices were put under the jurisdiction of Havana in 1733, the city became a magnet for wealth as it became more attractive to commerce and construction. With the founding of the University of Havana (*Real y Pontificia Universidad de Jerónimo de La Habana*) in 1728 by one of Cuba's "builder-bishops," Gerónimo Valdés, there was a surge of ecclesiastical construction. In addition to the churches, monasteries, and convents, private homes and palaces (*palacios*) were built. Private mansions such as Casa del Conde de San Juan Jaruco (1737), Casa del Marqués de Aguas Claras (1751), Casa del Marqués de Arcos (1746), and the Palacio del Conde Lombillo (1737) gave Havana the reputation of being the "City of Palaces." These eighteenth-century aristocratic palaces are testimony to the vast wealth amassed through commerce in slaves, tobacco, and sugar. In María Luisa Lobo Montalvo's description of the city, she explains how the cosmopolitan character of Havana influenced the whole island:

> During the first half of the eighteenth century, Havana—crossroads of the Indies—ceased to be a mere hub of American commerce, and became a thriving city, exporting the bounty of the tropics: tobacco (despite the state monopoly decreed in 1717), sugar, salted meat, hides, livestock, and hardwoods. It was an expensive city, where wages were higher than in Spain or Holland.[48]

OPPOSITE:
FIG. 68. A PAIR OF EARLY EIGHTEENTH-CENTURY CUBAN CHAIRS FLANK A LATER CUBAN SACRISTY CHEST. THE CHEST'S DESIGN, WITH ITS FANCIFUL BLOCKING AND CURVING FRONT, HAS BEEN ATTRIBUTED TO CUBAN CRAFTSMEN.

FIG. 69. DETAIL OF A HEAVY, PROTRUDING ROCOCO SCROLL FOOT ON THE SACRISTY CHEST SHOWN IN FIG. 68, WITH ITS ORNATE CARVED CARTOUCHE. CUBAN SACRISTY CHESTS WERE MADE OF ISLAND MAHOGANY (*CAOBA*), WITH CEDAR (*CEDRO*) FOR THE INTERIOR AND FOR OTHER SECONDARY WORK.

FIG. 70. LOUVERED SHUTTERS
AND WROUGHT-IRON RAILINGS
ARE STYLISTIC ELEMENTS THAT
DEFINE CUBAN BUILDINGS.

The eighteenth-century churches and palaces of Cuban cities were brought to life with a new architectural plasticity. Movement was chiseled into stone and typical Baroque two- and three-story façades were designed with colonnades, stucco, stained glass fanlights (*vitrales*), and statues. Alternating concave and convex planes with columns, pediments, niches, and volutes created illusory perspectives. This chiaroscuro effect provided contrast in the play of light and shade during the day.

The late seventeenth century had also seen the arrival of the Churrigueresque style. Named after Spanish architect José Churriguera (1664–1725), this style consisted of heavy, contorted ornamental decoration. It was found on a limited basis in the Spanish colonies, and was ultimately more popular in Mexico than in Cuba.

There is no better example of the Churrigueresque style than the Cathedral of Havana with its ornate, columned façade. Constructed of *coquina*, a fossilized coral rock (also known as "black teeth" or "ironshore") and limestone, it dominates Havana's Cathedral Plaza. Built in 1748 and completed in 1777, the cathedral is the island's monument to the ostentatious ornament of the Churrigueresque-influenced Cuban Baroque style and has been described by Cuban author Alejo Carpentier as "music turned into stone."

During the mid-eighteenth century, when the Spanish Bourbon monarch Charles III ("the Reformer's King") inherited the throne of Spain (1759), he found himself in the middle of the Seven Years' War (1750–63). In 1762, England declared war on Spain and France, and captured Havana. Havana and the western half of Cuba were ceded to England, and Havana became an open port, which inherently changed the social, economic, and political landscape of the island.

> *During the British occupation, Havana's residents had enjoyed their ability to purchase coveted consumer goods from the British merchants that had descended upon the city. With the return of Spanish rule, the government had instituted a degree of* comercio libre, *or free trade, which, while not the economic freedom of unrestricted laissez-faire, was a vast improvement over the previous system.*[49]

During the mid-eighteenth century, construction continued and Cuban buildings became more dynamic and decorative; the furnishings within them followed suit. The

coquina, *a fossilized coral rock, and limestone, it dominates Havana's Cathedral Plaza.*

later, more elaborate Baroque style revealed the beginnings of the French asymmetrical, embellished Rococo influence. Characterized by the fine exotic hardwoods and exuberant ornamentation both in turnings and carvings, Cuban furniture followed the architectonic design of the era.

> *Elements derived from Cuban architecture are often present in furniture dating from this period; the Baroque Havana jamb was frequently copied on cupboard crestings, cabinets and beds, while the relief work and fine moldings found on doors and window frames were used as surface decoration.*[50]

The occupants of the homes sought only the latest in the fineries of Europe and fashionable furnishings. With the new *comercio libre* (free trade policy), European furnishings were now imported either directly from France, England, or Holland, as well as from Spain. Consequently, the Cuban furniture crafted during this period adopted foreign forms and designs such as the Queen Anne style, as well as French and Dutch Baroque and Rococo elements more quickly. In an article about English eighteenth-century furniture exports to Spain, R.W. Symonds states:

> *London since earliest times had possessed the reputation for the making of articles of the best quality and of the latest design. Not only to Englishmen at home and in the colonies, but also to many foreigners …[t]he distinctive features of design, apart from the brighter coloring of the japan grounds, the use of cane seats to chairs, stools and settees owing to their greater coolness in a hot climate, is one noticeable characteristic of this furniture.*[51]

The most common and distinctive feature of Cuban furniture was its island mahogany construction. In Spain as well as in Europe, oak and walnut had been the most commonly used woods from the Renaissance until the first quarter of the eighteenth century, when mahogany became the preferred wood. In the mid-eighteenth century Cuba had the largest swietenia mahogany supply of the New World ports. The wood was plentiful, easily carved, dense, and close-grained, which allowed it to respond magnificently to varnishing and polishing according to the taste in design at the time. Like Cuba, Spain was also inundated with foreign fashions in furniture design and because of this, many scholars maintain that

any purity of form in Spanish furniture design had disappeared by the eighteenth century.

Spain gradually lost her national traits in furniture toward the end of the XVII century. In the XVIII they completely disappeared during the rule of the Bourbons, when the dominant styles were naturally those called "Louis," which in many cases were full of elegance and restlessness of line, whose curves and graces sharply conflicted with Spain's characteristic robustness and simplicity.[52]

What some furniture aficionados considered a loss for Spain was a gain for Cuba. While eighteenth-century foreign influences are considered a dilution of the integrity of Spanish furniture's sobriety and serenity, the majority of Cuban Baroque furniture forms are exuberant in their unique application of vernacular interpretation. Cuban artisans interpreted the exotic elements from the new colony and the different cultural influences unknown to Europe to create a diverse style of furniture that featured rich woods, bold proportions, and dramatic ornamentation.

Owing mainly to the increase in sugar cultivation, Cuba had, by the mid-eighteenth century, become the wealthiest and most developed island in the New World and was considered one of the world's largest suppliers of "white gold" or "sweet gold." By the end of the century, Cuba was producing over 35,000 tons of sugar each year, and was known as "the Caribbean's sugar bowl." Many of the island's wealthiest families, who were known as *sacarocracia,* or sugar aristocrats, contributed to Cuba's economic development, as well as to its renowned fashion and style. Consequently, the beginning of a new age of wealth in the mid-1700s brought about a rapid increase in economic activity, and the Cuban nobility imported French furniture in the style of Louis XV from France and Chippendale and Georgian furniture from England. Although European furniture was thought to have more prestige than local pieces, the European imported furniture was made of walnut or other European softwoods and soon fell victim to the humidity, tropical woodworm, and termites.

The arrival of these imported European furniture forms created a demand from Cubans for reproductions of the latest fashions, and with that demand came Cuban craftsmen's

FIG. 71. AN EIGHTEENTH-CENTURY MAHOGANY CUBAN LINEN PRESS IN THE ENGLISH STYLE. ENGLISH INFLUENCE WAS PREVALENT IN CUBA THROUGHOUT THE EIGHTEENTH CENTURY, BUT NEVER SO MUCH SO THAT A CUBAN-MADE PIECE COULD BE MISTAKEN FOR ENGLISH.

The Cuban sacristy chest, or cómoda de sacristía, with its undulating front, is the essential

FIG. 72. A SMALL EIGHTEENTH-
CENTURY CUBAN MAHOGANY
SACRISTY CHEST OF DRAWERS
IN THE CHURCH OF SAN
FRANCISCO DE ASÍS IN
HAVANA

copies and reinterpretations. Cuban cabinetmakers were also influenced by new design ideas found in imported pattern books, particularly Thomas Chippendale's *The Gentleman and Cabinet-Maker's Director*, printed in 1754. This pattern book was the most comprehensive collection of popular furniture designs of the day, and its influence spread throughout Europe (the third edition was published in French), North America, and other British colonies. Gothic and Chinese ornamentation was featured along with the most popular French modern, or Rococo style.

> *During the eighteenth century master craftsmen, varnishers, and gilders flourished, many of Creole or Spanish origin. Foreign craftsmen introduced many new decorative techniques, and furniture inventories of the period describe numerous pieces embellished with inlays, marquetry and gilding. Wicker work was sometimes used for seat furniture.*[53]

One example of the new ornateness in style is the Cuban sacristy chest (*cómoda de sacristía*). The Spanish colonial sacristy chest was believed by many furniture scholars to have originated in Mexico but recent research points to a Cuban origin. Influenced by the English chest of drawers and the French Rococo-style commode, the sacristy chest, with its undulating surface, is the quintessential expression in a furniture form of the eighteenth-century Cuban Baroque and later, the Rococo. The French-style chest of drawers, or *commode*, was fully developed in Europe by the end of the seventeenth century. It wasn't until the second quarter of the eighteenth century that the form became popular in Cuba and furniture-makers there began to craft chests of drawers or commodes to replace the boxes and trunks that Cubans had used until that time.

Historically, the sacristy chest originated in Spain in the fifteenth century as a large architectural fitting that backed up to, or was built into, a wall of a church sacristy, a room behind or to the side of the altar used for the storage of sacred vessels and ecclesiastical robes. Originally the sacristy cupboard or chest held everything used in the celebration of mass (chalices, censers, patens, etc.) including the priest's vestments. Wealthy members of local congregations spent exorbitant amounts of money building and furnishing their churches. During the Baroque period, the churches, retables, choirs, altars, and sacristies were fabricated without limits of expense. Two examples of this are the very grand

expression in furniture of the eighteenth-century island Baroque style, and later, of the Rococo.

mahogany sacristy chests in the Cathedral of Havana and Espiritu Santo Church. Both were made of Cuban mahogany and cedar, one over twenty-three feet wide, the other over thirty feet wide. These block-front sacristy chests were crafted during the first half of the eighteenth century and are consistent with the other documented cabinetry work throughout the church and cathedral's sacristies.

Donors who gave generously to the construction of local churches commissioned the cabinetmakers to create smaller sacristy chests for their urban mansions. The chest was thus considered one of the *pièces de résistance* of any collection of furniture belonging to a member of Cuba's elite class, which was known to flaunt its wealth in typically nouveau-riche fashion. Made smaller and freestanding with block fronts, these extravagant chests mimicked the grand, ostentatious pieces first built into church sacristy walls, and the very possession of this adaptation of what was originally a religious form gave the owner an increased sense of importance. Influenced both by European imports and the desire to

OPPOSITE:
FIG. 77. AN IMPOSING COLO-
NIAL CUBAN *PALACIO* COURT-
YARD

BELOW:
FIG. 76. THE COURTYARD OF A
MANSION BUILT IN THE LAST
QUARTER OF THE EIGHTEENTH
CENTURY AND FIRST OCCUPIED
BY CUBA'S GOVERNOR, DON
LUIS DE LAS CASAS. THE
STATUE OF CHRISTOPHER
COLUMBUS IS BY THE ITALIAN
SCULPTOR CUCCHIARI.

transpose a piece of church furniture (the sacristy chest) from its original setting to their private residences, the Creole (*criolla*) aristocracy thus made the kind of statement on which the society of the day thrived. Sacristy chests were first commissioned by Cuban aristocrats, but as time went on they were ordered by everybody with pretensions to social position or wealth.

> *Technical developments during the eighteenth century led to a marked increase in the repertory of available furniture, and this diversity created richer ensembles to equip fashionable interiors. New items recorded in contemporary documents include large mirrors, musical instruments, and elaborate lamps. Traditional pieces of furniture were superseded: chests were replaced by chests-of-drawers; desks and writing tables by bureaux; and multi-chairback settees evolved. Cupboards used for both clothes and household goods proliferated.*[54]

The first Cuban sacristy chests were made of mahogany and were less elaborate than later examples, but they were Baroque in appearance nonetheless, with serpentine-shaped fronts. They were usually designed with three or four long drawers, which were block-front. As a rule, the drawer-front or block-front was cut from a single piece of wood and carved in a manner so as to form a repeating convex/concave surface. (Later in the eighteenth and nineteenth centuries the raised surface was sometimes attached by glue.) As the century progressed and the fashion of the French Rococo became more popular, the chests took on exceptionally sumptuous designs; the serpentine patterns on the chest fronts were continued on the sides and the feet protruded farther forward and had more deeply scrolled ends. The fronts of the more elaborate sacristy chests are reminiscent of the ornate curves and counter-curves of the previously mentioned Cathedral of Havana's façade.

The Cuban sacristy chest inspired craftsmen throughout the New World to copy versions of the piece; similar examples can be found throughout Mexico and South America. Whether the sacristy chest originated exclusively in Cuba or was designed concurrently throughout the New

FIG. 78. EIGHTEENTH-CENTURY
MAHOGANY CUBAN CHAIR WITH
DISTINCT ENGLISH CHARACTER-
ISTICS, INCLUDING CABRIOLE
LEGS, BALL-AND-CLAW FEET,
AND A VASIFORM BACK SPLAT

OPPOSITE:
FIG. 79. THE MAHOGANY-
PANELED LIBRARY IN LA DOLCE
DINORA, THE HAVANA HOME OF
THE TWENTIETH-CENTURY
CUBAN WRITER AND POLITICIAN
ORESTES FERRARA, DISPLAYS
BOTH SPANISH AND CUBAN
FURNITURE OF DIFFERENT
PERIODS.

OVERLEAF:
FIG. 80. THE HALL OF MIRRORS
IN THE EIGHTEENTH-CENTURY
PALACIO DE LOS CAPITANES
GENERALES IN HAVANA, WITH
A MIXTURE OF EUROPEAN AND
CUBAN FURNITURE AND
CRYSTAL CHANDELIERS

World is indeterminable at this point. Rococo Portuguese examples are found in Brazil and Dutch-bombé-inspired examples are found along the northern coast of South America near the Dutch islands of Curaçao, Aruba, and Bonaire. Many examples are also found in the urban centers of Mexico, particularly in Veracruz, Mexico City, and Puebla.

Although there were inventories of Cuban sacristy chests that were shipped throughout the Caribbean, there is no way of knowing if these chests were the prototypes for the aforementioned South American and Mexican pieces. "During the eighteenth century, Cuban furniture, notably chests-of-drawers, gained wide acceptance throughout Hispanic America."[55]

North American furniture scholars claim that block-front furniture design is an American innovation and that it originated in Newport, Rhode Island, with the cabinetmakers John Townsend and John Goddard in the 1760s. More recent research places the earliest known block-front form in Boston in the 1740s. However, the serpentine block-front sacristy chests made in Cuba were also built in the 1740s, as documented, a fact that casts doubt on the theories of a North American origin for the block-front style. There is so far no evidence to show how the block-front style was transmitted from Cuba to Boston, but there *are* shipping records of merchants who visited Havana to select and purchase island mahogany for cabinetmaking.

Armoires or wardrobes (*roperos*), like the chests of drawers, were also used for storage. Originally the armoire was a cupboard used as a repository for arms during the Gothic period in France. During the Renaissance it came to be used as storage for personal clothing and household possessions. During the late sixteenth and seventeenth centuries, Cuban armoires were rather plain and undecorated. The few elaborate armoires from this period were either imported from Spain or made for church use. However, as with sacristy chests, Cuba's wealthy elite soon desired the form for their residences, and, beginning in the eighteenth century, armoires were commissioned for private use. As these tall, rectilinear armoires became more plentiful, they also became more decorative. In order to maintain their mobility, large armoires were designed to be disassembled into sections; typically these sections were the cornice, base, two doors, two sides, and the boards that make up the back panel.

Another form believed by some furniture scholars to have originated in Cuba during the eighteenth century is the leather sling-seat lolling armchair, often referred to as a "planter's chair," "Spanish chair," or "Campeche chair." The origin of this low-slung chair with an

but in the eighteenth century, private owners commissioned more lavishly decorated examples.

inclined seat is obscure, although recent scholarship has shown that the Cuban planter's chair is a Spanish innovation that combined the curule base with a leather sling-seat.

> *The unusual form of this chair, variously called a "lolling chair," "siesta chair," "Spanish chair," or "campeachy," had its origins in ancient Egypt. Versions of the design with its characteristic X-shaped stretchers were known in ancient Greece and Rome and were fashionable in France and Spain during the seventeenth century. The campeachy form that was popular in New Orleans was apparently derived from Spanish sources. The name "campeachy" is an anglicized spelling of Campeche, a Mexican state, where a kind of mahogany called "bloodwood" or "logwood" was grown, which was often used to make the chair.*[56]

Many examples are found in Cuba (where it is referred to as a planter's chair, Havana chair or smoker's chair), Jamaica (Spanish chair), and Mexico and Louisiana (Campeche chair). The oldest known example of this chair form is said to have originated in the Canary Islands and is now in the March collection, a private collection on Mallorca, in the Balearic Islands off Spain. Scholars had previously dated this chair from the seventeenth century, but recent research has more correctly dated it as early to mid-eighteenth century.

> *The influence of Baroque design is made manifest in the elaborately carved, shell-shaped rail and curvilinear arms of this chair. A more accurate date for the March chair would be mid-eighteenth century, based on these interpretive details.*[57]

Determining a piece of furniture's country of origin is made all the more difficult by the fact that missionaries, government officials, and wealthy planters often took their furniture (or sent it on) to their next posting, or brought it home with them when they returned to Europe. Because furniture was transported back and forth from Spain to the New World and its colonies, wood analysis is required on the early March collection chair to determine its place of origin—whether Spain, the Balearic Islands, Canary Islands, Cuba, Mexico, or some other part of the New World.

Although the Cuban version of the planter's chair is unmistakably an island innovation, the eighteenth-century leather sling-seat lolling chair is unquestionably of

Spanish design and craftsmanship. Of all the different interpretations of the form, the Filipino *silla perezosa* (lazy chair), a variation on the country's similar and more common *butaca* chair, is most like the Cuban lolling and Jamaican Spanish chairs. This similarity further strengthens the argument for the Spanish origin of not only the Cuban chair, but also of the West Indian planter's chair.

If quantity were the only determining factor for the origin of the form, then Cuba would certainly be the first choice, since so many examples are found on the island. Throughout the colonial era, the Cuban planter's chair was used exclusively by men, which is why it may have been called a "smoker's chair" during the nineteenth century. Many similar "down island" (more southern Caribbean islands) planter's chairs are caned rather than fitted with leather or cloth sling seats. Although caning was gaining popularity in the Caribbean because of its ability to facilitate airflow and keep the sitter cool, caned planter's chairs are rare in Cuba. Hundreds of the leather Havana smoker's chairs are found throughout Cuba, most made of mahogany and easily stylistically dated from the mid-eighteenth to early twentieth century. Some have been made of heavier wood such as greenheart, sabicu, bullet-wood, or logwood, and have embossed decorative leather seats. Logwood is an indigenous wood that grew along Cuba's coast and was one of the first woods cut and traded by the Spaniards. Also known as campeche wood, it was valuable for its dyeing capabilities (and sometimes called dyewood). Although not as easily worked as mahogany or sabicu, it was used in Cuban cabinetry. Whether the use of campeche wood in some Cuban planter's chairs contributed to their nomenclature (as "campeche chairs") remains undetermined. According to a number of Cuban furniture scholars, there was an immigration of Mexican woodworkers from Campeche, called *Campechanos,* to Cuba. These woodworkers produced a version of the form in Cuba and subsequently the Cuban form is sometimes referred to as a Campeche chair.

There are many similar examples of the same form—and called Spanish chairs—found in the nearby island of Jamaica, particularly on the north shore of the island (closest to Cuba), and in and around the seventeenth-century Spanish capital of Jamaica, Port Royal, once known as "the wickedest city in the West" or "the Sodom of the Indies." There are also many examples found a few miles inland, at Spanish Town (the former Spanish city of Santiago de la Vega). More variations of the planter's chair are found throughout the West Indies, with

FIG. 83. A PAIR OF NINE-
TEENTH-CENTURY MAHOGANY
AND LEATHER CUBAN PLANTA-
TION OR SMOKER'S CHAIRS,
OFTEN CALLED CAMPECHE
CHAIRS

extended arms used as leg and foot rests. Many of the "down island" West Indian chairs are caned, unlike those in Cuba. Caned Cuban examples were not made until the late nineteenth or early twentieth century.

Eventually the Spanish and Cuban nobility's desire for generous proportions (which was allowed by the endless supply of mahogany) and more elaborate display influenced the craftsmen to produce copies less faithful to the European originals. The monumental proportions and deeper, more elaborate carvings on chairs, chests, and table legs were far more exotic and exaggerated than those of their European counterparts. From the mid- to late eighteenth century, Cuban furniture reached the apogee of design and craftsmanship.

As the Cuban Baroque furnishings took on a more embellished ornamentation and became Rococo with asymmetrical S- and C-scrolls and cartouche motifs, fashion reacted against the overly elaborate designs. By the 1780s and 1790s, the fussiness of the Rococo style had become less favored. In furniture, as in art, there are no abrupt style changes; one style overlaps another and gradually replaces it. Prompted by the eighteenth-century archaeological discoveries at Pompeii and Herculaneum, European designers were the first

to produce larger and more elaborately carved furniture than their European counterparts.

to introduce the Neoclassical movement. Eventually taste changed, and Neoclassicism and its straight, measured lines and Classical decorative motifs came into fashion, particularly among Cuba's urbanites. The transitional period of the 1780s and 1790s mixed Rococo curvilinear extravagances with the straight lines of the Neoclassical Period. Design lines gradually became more symmetrical and Classical proportions were adopted. By the early 1800s, the Rococo S-curve had completely given way to severe, Classical straightness and symmetry in design.

During the last half of the eighteenth century, even larger religious, secular, and governmental buildings were erected. One such example is the Palacio de los Capitánes Generales in Havana in the Plaza de Armas Carlos Manuel de Céspedes, an outstanding example of Cuban urban architecture from the third quarter of the eighteenth century. Felipe de Fonsdeoviela, Marqués de la Torre, who was Capitán General of the island of Cuba from 1771 to 1776, hired Cuban architect Antonio Fernandez de Trebejos to design and engineer the building. The construction, which took eighteen years, was inaugurated in 1791. Typical of the palatial townhouses built by Cuban oligarchic families, it is also one of the most elegant late Baroque buildings with Neoclassical elements in Havana. It served as the residence of Cuba's colonial governors. Much of the furniture in the Palacio de los Capitánes Generales is late eighteenth- and early nineteenth-century, a combination of imported and Cuban-made pieces, which is representative of the period.

During the last quarter of the eighteenth century, the Spanish Bourbon monarch Charles III (1759–1808) continued to rule Spain with "Bourbon enlightenment." Consequently, Cuba's wealthy Creole class began to feel alienated from the mother country, which, during the nineteenth century, ultimately drove the colony toward a desire for independence.

FIG. 84. CUBAN "SMOKER'S CHAIRS" LIKE THIS MAHOGANY AND CANE ONE WERE POPULAR DURING THE NINETEENTH CENTURY. THE ARM FEATURES AN ATTACHED METAL ASH TRAY AND CIGAR HOLDER.

FIG. 85. A PAIR OF EARLY NINE-TEENTH-CENTURY "SMOKER'S CHAIRS." THESE ARE CUBA'S VERSION OF THE CARIBBEAN PLANTER'S CHAIR, BOTH WITH CURULE BASES AND LEATHER SLING SEATS.

95

FIG. 86. EIGHTEENTH-
CENTURY-STYLE CUBAN
MAHOGANY FURNITURE MADE
FOR THE BEDROOM IN EAST-
ERN CUBA. HERE THE BED
AND SMALL STAND FEATURE
CARVED PROTRUDING
SCROLLED FEET.

FIG. 87. AN EIGHTEENTH-
CENTURY CUBAN ARMOIRE
(*ARMARIO*) MADE IN THE
ENGLISH CHIPPENDALE STYLE.
THE SECONDARY WOOD IS
INDIGENOUS ISLAND CEDAR;
THE CONSTRUCTION IS
UNMISTAKABLY CUBAN.

97

Chapter IV   TOWARD INDEPENDENCE: THE NINETEENTH CENTURY

FIG. 88. *AZULEJOS*, OR TILES, WERE AN ESSENTIAL DECORATIVE ELEMENT IN CUBAN ARCHITECTURE. SPANISH CERAMIC TILES PAINTED WITH MOORISH-INSPIRED PATTERNS WERE SHIPPED TO CUBA, WHERE THEY ADORNED THE WALLS AND FLOORS OF BUILDINGS SUCH AS THIS NINETEENTH-CENTURY PRIVATE HOME IN TRINIDAD.

For most of the Caribbean islands, the nineteenth century was a period of gradual neglect, poverty, and decay. For Cuba it was a century of continual and progressive prosperity as it grew increasingly more sophisticated and elegant. The wealthy plantation owners and merchants built larger mansions with late Baroque, Rococo, and Neoclassical elements and filled them with the latest furnishings.

The nineteenth century was an epoch of romance. Its history in Cuba is packed with proud patricians who dueled with one another over minute points of honor or conspired for the ideals of equality and freedom; who were capable of emancipating their slaves and giving up huge fortunes to take up arms against the Metropolis, offering their lives for the motherland.[58]

Cuba had made great economic strides in its commercial development by the end of the eighteenth century. The slave revolt of 1791 in Saint-Dominique, Cuba's biggest rival in sugar production (its name was changed to Haiti when the western third of Hispaniola gained formal independence in 1804), was a tremendous boost to the Cuban sugar industry. Up to that point, the French had con-

trolled three quarters of the European sugar market. With the advent of the revolt, French sugar and coffee planter émigrés fled to Cuba, which made Cuba the main sugar producer and slave importer in the Caribbean, and gave the island a much larger portion of the international sugar market.

Finally, many exiles fled from Saint Domingue to Cuba, particularly to the neighborhood of Santiago, but also to other places in the island. These exiles brought with them not only the passepied *and the* contredance, *the powdered wig and Parisian dress (and the French habit of turning their feet outward to show off their slippers), but also terrible stories of rape, murder, looting and destruction which were enough to keep Cuban planters from giving an inch to their slaves for nearly a hundred years.*[59]

Unlike other European countries, Spain did not issue emancipation until late in the century, which was one of the primary reasons Cuba continued to grow commercially.

Opposite and left: Figs. 89 and 90. The streets of old Havana were filled with *volantes*, small one-horse carriages with leather tops and enormous wheels, driven by postilions in high Spanish leather boots.

Below: fig. 91. The eighteenth-century House of the Conde de Santovenía on the Plaza de Armas in Havana. The Tuscan-like columns flank arched windows with colored glass fanlights.

FIG. 92. THE SUGAR ARISTO-
CRATS, OR *SACAROCRACIA*,
WERE RESPONSIBLE FOR
IMPORTING NOT ONLY SPANISH
AND FRENCH FURNITURE, BUT
ENGLISH FURNITURE AS WELL.
THIS INTRICATELY CARVED
EIGHTEENTH-CENTURY CON-
SOLE IS ONE OF A PAIR OF
ENGLISH PIECES WITH A HIS-
TORY OF HAVING BEEN IN
CUBA SINCE THE EARLY 1800S.

FIG. 93. BUILT-IN MAHOGANY
CABINET DOORS WITH CIRCU-
LAR LOUVERED OPENINGS
TO ALLOW AIRFLOW AND ELE-
GANT FRESCOES DECORATE
THE RECEPTION ROOMS IN
THE PALACIO BRUNET, BUILT
IN 1812 AS THE RESIDENCE
OF THE WEALTHY BORRELL
FAMILY IN TRINIDAD.

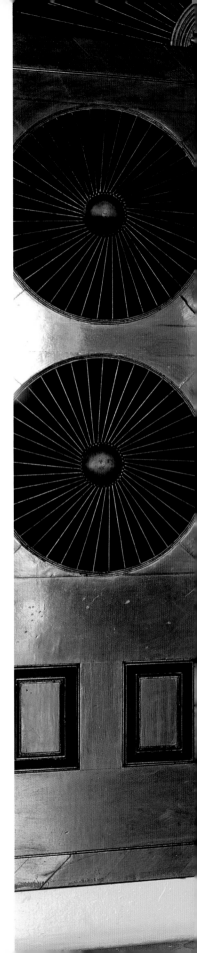

This free-labor plantocracy allowed Cuba's sugar estates to thrive while other Caribbean islands' economies failed. In Cuba, sugar was king and the number of sugar mills (*ingenios*) multiplied. In the early 1800s, there were over 500 sugar mills. By the 1830s, Cuba had not only become the world's largest sugar producer but the world's richest colony as well, and by mid-century the number of sugar mills had tripled to over 1500. In 1851, Cuba produced six million hundredweight of sugar, more than twice the production of all the English Caribbean islands that year. Although sugar was the engine that drove the economy, Cuba's elite (both peninsular and Creole) were not simply sugar producers (sugar cultivation and plantation slavery); they also followed a variety of other economic pursuits: mercantile shipping, landholding, and agriculture (coffee, cotton, and tobacco).

> *Sugar threw Cuba open to the world, and the world came to Cuba. A large number of foreigners with an interest in the slave trade or other business settled here. They were followed, for brief or long stays, by a bevy of foreign artists and craftsmen-musicians, engravers, painters, sculptors, architects, goldsmiths, iron-smiths, and many others—mostly from England, Italy, France and the United States.*[60]

With the infusion of new people and new ideas came the spread of a new aesthetic and new fashions. Inter-colonial trade brought more furniture styles from "down island" (English, Danish, French, and Dutch). As previously mentioned, by the nineteenth century the Baroque and Rococo architectural styles in the Spanish Greater Antilles eventually fell from favor and were succeeded by the more fashionable Classical symmetry of the Neoclassical style. The Neoclassical "sugar palaces" boasted Classical façades with pediments and engaged pilasters, internal patios, galleried arcades, and balconies with carved arches.

Throughout the nineteenth century, Spain's colonial independence persisted and wealth continued to increase. The colony's architecture became more opulent than ever and ranged in style with elements of Mudéjar, Colonial Baroque, and Rococo combined with the predominant Neoclassical style. In a description of a typical nineteenth-century Havana mansion or *palacete*, María Luisa Lobo states:

> *Marble floors replaced the old, dark pavements of tile. The main staircase touched unprecedented heights of monumentality, splendor of design, and richness of material. Finally, the court was converted into a central ornamental component, becoming filled with fountains, statues, benches, flowering plants, and shrubs. The house thus appeared transformed, even though little had changed in structural terms. In short, these were mansions fit for elegant, gracious living, complemented by superb furniture.*[61]

Furniture from the beginning of this period also reflected the new Classical and Empire styles, which were thoroughly assimilated into the island's architectural vernacular. Furniture continued to be imported both by order and as "venture" cargo. Although early shipping references to North American furniture shipping are limited, Nancy McClelland recorded that $63,000 worth of furniture was delivered to Cuba in 1821.[62]

From 1810 to 1830, wars for independence reigned throughout Latin American colonies and caused a migration of Spanish loyalists to relocate to Cuba. Cuba became officially recognized as the "Ever-Faithful Isle." Although colonial dependence on Spain persisted during the last quarter of the eighteenth and through the nineteenth century, the Neoclassical style came to Cuba from trade with North America as well as with Spain and Europe. One of Cuba's best examples of Neoclassicism is the Palacio de Justo Cantero in Trinidad, constructed between 1828 and 1830 for a wealthy Catalonian family, and regarded as one of the island's most luxurious Neoclassical buildings. Legend has it that the nineteenth-century owner acquired his vast sugar estates by poisoning a prominent slave trader and marrying his widow, who also died mysteriously soon thereafter.

The furniture throughout the mansion is of the period and in keeping with what has been found in homes during the first half of the 1800s.

> *The old families of Trinidad had become extremely rich during the first decades of the nineteenth century, and frequently had their furniture brought over from Europe or the United States. Many of these imported pieces were copied by local craftsmen and were to be seen in all of Cuba's most opulent homes.*[63]

As the first decades of the nineteenth century progressed, late Neoclassical and Empire style furniture became heavier as the use of mahogany and mahogany veneer became more prevalent. Adolfo de Hostos described an early nineteenth-century Spanish colonial room:

> *Up to the 1830s, the parlor would be equipped with heavy furniture of solid mahogany, all elaborately carved: marble-topped pedestal tables, chairs upholstered in horse hair or leather, and folding game tables. For the bedrooms enormous mahogany double beds with four turned posts were imported from Curaçao, or field beds were fitted with wooden frames above for curtains or mosquito nets; later metal beds were imported from Europe. Large mahogany wardrobes and chests of*

FIG. 106. CUBAN HAND-
CRAFTED CARVING FROM THE
MID-NINETEENTH CENTURY

OPPOSITE:
FIG. 103. ONE OF THE BED-
ROOMS FROM THE PALACIO DE
LOS CAPITANES GENERALES,
WITH VARIOUS EUROPEAN
PAINTINGS AND CUBAN-MADE
FURNITURE

LEFT, ABOVE:
FIG. 104. A NINETEENTH-
CENTURY BEDROOM WITH A
CUBAN-MADE RENAISSANCE-
REVIVAL SUITE OF MAHOGANY
FURNITURE

LEFT, BELOW:
FIG. 105. PART OF THE COL-
LECTION OF THE CUBAN
MILLIONAIRE JULIO LOBO IS IN
THIS ROOM FURNISHED WITH
FRENCH EMPIRE FURNITURE.
LEGEND HAS IT THAT NAPOLEON
BONAPARTE ACTUALLY SLEPT
IN THIS BED SOMETIME BEFORE
LOBO PURCHASED IT AND
BROUGHT IT TO CUBA.

111

The mahogany and cane rocking chair, copied from the North American rocker, was hugely

popular in Cuba. By the 1830s, it could be found in homes and offices throughout the island.

drawers matched the bedsteads. Other amenities acquired in the first third of the 1800s include glass hanging lanterns and table lanterns, brass and silver candlesticks and hurricane shades, shelf clocks, Sèvres porcelain vases, silver tableware, large framed mirrors, books, and keyboard instruments.[64]

With the conclusion of the Neoclassical style in the late 1820s in Havana (and a decade later in the provincial towns), a similar but heavier, more plain, fashion emerged: the Cuban Empire, or *Imperio* style. This style was synonymous with the Regency style in England and with the Empire style in France. Throughout the eighteenth century, it usually took from ten to twenty years for a new furniture style from Europe or North America to filter down to Cuba and become popular. This was not the case in the nineteenth century with the Empire style and its heavier-designed cousin the Classical Revival style, both of which became fashionable immediately.

One of the most popular expressions of nineteenth-century Cuban furniture is the mahogany and cane rocking chair, copied from the North American form. The North American rocking chair probably evolved from having rockers fitted to the legs of a chair (possibly inspired by cradles) in the first half of the eighteenth century. By the 1830s, the form had reached Cuba and become so popular that it was found not only in the finest of homes, government and merchants offices but in middle-class homes as well. The first Cuban rocking chairs have Empire- or Classical-Revival-designed lines and are always caned and made of mahogany. The open work caning enables the sitter to stay cool by rocking.

The rocker suited the Cuban temperament to perfection. It was constantly evoked by travelers who were bewitched by the image of Havana beauties rocking back and forth, lazily fanning themselves beside trays of cool drinks and tropical fruit.[65]

One of the reasons that caning became very fashionable in Cuban seating furniture during this period was due to its popularity in Europe. Military use of campaign furniture (which featured caning) during the Napoleonic Wars (1793–1815) enhanced its popularity. Although fashionable in Europe for its exotic decorative effect, caning had the added appeal of practicality in Cuba's tropical climate. Adolfo de Hostos records:

FIG. 108. A CUBAN-MADE MAHOGANY DESK. CURVILINEAR BAROQUE MOTIFS WERE POPULAR THROUGHOUT CUBA'S COLONIAL PERIOD, EVEN AT THE TURN OF THE NINETEENTH CENTURY.

OPPOSITE:
FIG. 107. HALL OF THE TOWN COUNCIL (*SALA DEL CABILDO*) OF HAVANA IN THE PALACIO DE LOS CAPITÁNES GENERALES. THE FURNITURE IS CUBAN-MADE OF ISLAND MAHOGANY.

FIG. 110. A DETAIL OF THE
CUBAN COLONIAL EMPIRE
CONSOLE, SHOWING THE HIGH
QUALITY OF CUBAN CARVING

FIG. 109. AN EARLY NINE-
TEENTH-CENTURY CUBAN
CONSOLE MADE OF ISLAND
MAHOGANY, FLANKED BY A PAIR
OF MAHOGANY AND CANE
CUBAN COLONIAL EMPIRE
HIGH-BACK ARMCHAIRS

OPPOSITE:
FIG. 111. CUBAN *PALACIOS*
CONTAINED A MIXTURE OF
EUROPEAN PERIOD FURNISH-
INGS AND CUBAN-MADE
PIECES. SEATING FURNITURE
WAS ADAPTED TO THE TROPI-
CAL HEAT, WITH CANING USED
IN PLACE OF UPHOLSTERY.

FIG. 112. NEOCLASSICAL ARCHITECTURAL ELEMENTS WERE POPULAR IN CUBA FROM THE LATE EIGHTEENTH CENTURY THROUGHOUT THE NINETEENTH CENTURY. MANY HOMES, SUCH AS THIS PRIVATE RESIDENCE, INCORPORATED THESE POPULAR NEOCLASSICAL ELEMENTS.

FIG. 113. A SMALL INTERIOR PATIO IN AN URBAN HOME WITH A RUSTIC NINETEENTH-CENTURY MAHOGANY BENCH IN THE EARLY SPANISH COLONIAL STYLE.

FIG. 114. ONE OF THE MOST
LUXURIOUS PAINTED ROOMS IN
CUBA. THIS LAVISH NEOCLAS-
SICAL RECEPTION ROOM HAS A
CARRARA MARBLE FLOOR AND
IS DELINEATED BY ARCADES TO
FACILITATE AIRFLOW.

FIG. 115. TYPICAL OF CUBAN
DRAWING ROOMS ARE CANED
CHAIRS (IN MANY CASES
ROCKERS) GROUPED AROUND
CENTER TABLES, WHERE THE
CROSS-FLOW OF TROPICAL
BREEZES FROM DOORS AND
WINDOWS CAN PROVIDE
COOL AIR.

FIG. 116. THIS ROOM IN
SANTIAGO DE CUBA IS TYPICAL
OF WHAT MIGHT BE FOUND IN
AN EARLY NINETEENTH-CEN-
TURY CUBAN HOUSE, WITH ITS
PERIOD CUBAN FURNITURE
AND IMPORTED CRYSTAL.

About the mid 1830s caned furniture, so practical and comfortable in the tropics, came increasingly into use. The Neo-Rococo forms that in northern regions were generously cushioned and upholstered with horsehair or velvet were fitted with caning in round or oval carved mahogany frames and usually protected by antimacassars. Less expensive seats, though also of mahogany had backs and seats of rush.[66]

Muebles de Medallón is a term that refers to seating furniture that incorporated carved medallion-shape seats and backs, which was popular from the mid- to late 1800s in Cuba. Mahogany and cane furniture in the revival styles (Classical, Rococo, and Renaissance) was produced in suites in Cuba and the other Spanish Antilles. Cuba's Rococo-revival *medallón* style proliferated and was the most popular of all the revival styles on the island. Another popular revival style frequently copied was the Renaissance revival style, with its geometric patterns and carved Classical decorative motifs. Both styles were popular until the turn of the twentieth century.

With the nineteenth century came steam power and the arrival of the industrial revolution in Cuba. The capability of manufacturing furniture by machine to produce multiples relatively inexpensively enabled companies to export thousands of pieces of furniture. Cuba was now not only an importer of the foreign made furniture but a manufacturer as well. Small cabinetmaking shops grew and new companies capable of machine production started to make furniture in varying degrees of elegance and sophistication.

The succession of furniture styles in nineteenth-century Cuba corresponded to the sequence of styles not only in Europe at the time, but in North America as well. Only ninety miles from the North American southern coast, American fashion and culture became a formidable influence on Cuban taste.

An increase in trade with both Europe and North America was responsible for the influx of the many revival styles popular during the century. Examples in Cuba show a direct relationship between nineteenth-century imported prototype pieces and the island copies. In

OPPOSITE:
FIG. 119. PART OF THE EARLY
NINETEENTH-CENTURY
NAPOLEONIC COLLECTION
OF THE SUGAR TRADER JULIO
LOBO Y OLAVARRIA

LEFT, TOP:
FIG. 120. EXAMPLES OF EARLY
NINETEENTH-CENTURY FRENCH
IMPERIAL-STYLE FURNITURE
IMPORTED TO CUBA

LEFT, BELOW:
FIG. 121. A PAINTING BY JEAN
VIBERT SHOWING NAPOLEON
PREPARING FOR HIS CORONA-
TION IS HUNG ABOVE A FRENCH
EMPIRE COMMODE. THE ELAB-
ORATE HAND-WROUGHT IRON
GATE IS A TYPICAL CUBAN
ELEMENT.

OVERLEAF LEFT:
FIG. 122. THIS EIGHTEENTH-
CENTURY MAHOGANY AND SAT-
INWOOD DESK IS ONE OF MANY
EARLY IMPORTED NORTH
AMERICAN FURNITURE PIECES
IN CUBA TODAY.

OVERLEAF RIGHT:
FIG. 123. THE DECOR OF THIS
MID-EIGHTEENTH-CENTURY
PALACIO REVEALS THE CUBAN
ARISTOCRACY'S PASSION FOR
BOTH IMPORTED AND CUBAN-
MADE FURNISHINGS. THIS
ROOM FEATURES A CARRARA
MARBLE FLOOR, SÈVRES
PORCELAIN, NEOCLASSICAL
MURALS, AND ISLAND-MADE
MAHOGANY FURNITURE.

fact the illustrated catalogue of 1881 issued by J. W. Mason and Company in New York City contained a preface addressed "To Merchants and Dealers" that was printed in English as well as in Spanish. Stylistic transfer occurred through the importation of the printed catalogue as well as of the actual pieces of North American and European furniture. There are no private records available from Cuban cabinet shops from the nineteenth century, but there were sufficient quantities of island-made furniture that show close adherence to imported prototypes, which prove that these served as an inspiration and model for patrons and craftsmen. The origin of nineteenth-century Spanish colonial furniture pieces is often difficult to identify because of their close similarity to imported models. However, if both the primary and the secondary woods are mahogany (imports were hardly ever made of mahogany), and if the wood is turned and carved by hand rather than by machine, it is safe to assume that it is an island-made piece.

Many advertisements appeared in Cuban newspapers announcing the arrival of ships from the north with cargoes of furniture. The low price of imported furniture inevitably accelerated demand, and this factor had a powerful influence on Cuban craftsmanship; spectacular items of carved and inlaid furniture were produced as the industry expanded and diversified. [67]

FIG. 125. A CEILING FRESCO IN THE TEATRO TOMÁS TERRY IN CIENFUEGOS. THE THEATER WAS BUILT IN 1886 BY THE SUGAR AND SLAVE TRADER TOMÁS TERRY ADAMS. WORLD-FAMOUS ENTERTAINERS SUCH AS SARAH BERNHARDT AND ENRICO CARUSO PERFORMED HERE.

OPPOSITE:
FIG. 124. PART OF THE COLLECTION OF NAPOLEONICA FROM JULIO LOBO'S SALÓN, NOW IN HAVANA'S NAPOLEONIC MUSEUM. THIS COLLECTION INCLUDES FURNITURE AND DECORATIVE ARTS THAT BELONGED TO THE FRENCH EMPEROR.

LEFT:
FIG. 126. THE THRONE ROOM IN THE PALACIO DE LOS CAPITÁNES GENERALES. NEVER USED BY A SPANISH MONARCH, THE THRONE OF HAVANA WAS A SYMBOL OF GOVERNMENT FROM AFAR.

FIG. 128. THIS LATE EIGH-
TEENTH-CENTURY CUBAN-
MADE MAHOGANY CHINA
CABINET WITH FANNED
MEDIOPUNTO WAS BUILT INTO
THE WALL BETWEEN THE
DINING AND LIVING ROOM,
ALLOWING FOR BETTER
VENTILATION THROUGHOUT
THE ROOMS.

OPPOSITE:
FIG. 127. A DECORATED TILE
AZULEJO ENTRANCE HALL TO A
PRIVATE HOME, WITH HIGH
CEILINGS AND COLORED GLASS
MAMPARAS, WHICH ASSURE
COMFORT IN THE TROPICAL
HEAT

OVERLEAF LEFT:
FIG. 129. A TYPICAL EARLY
NINETEENTH-CENTURY BED-
ROOM IN SANTIAGO DE CUBA,
WITH A CUBAN MAHOGANY
SLEIGH BED

OVERLEAF RIGHT:
FIG. 130. SEATING FURNITURE
WAS ADAPTED TO CUBA'S TROP-
ICAL HEAT, WITH COOLER
OPEN CANING USED IN PLACE
OF TAPESTRY OR UPHOLSTERY.
THIS CUBAN EMPIRE CHAIR'S
DESIGN, WITH ITS HIGH BACK,
CABRIOLE LEGS, AND KLISMOS
CRESTRAIL, IS NOT FOUND ON
ANY CARIBBEAN ISLAND
EXCEPT CUBA.

FIG. 131. A SOPHISTICATED
EARLY NINETEENTH-CENTURY
MAHOGANY *TINAJERO,* OR
WATER FILTER, WITH JARS TO
HOLD THE WATER AND A FILTER
OF POROUS STONE

FIG. 132. LUXURIOUS BATH-
ROOMS WITH LARGE MARBLE
BATHTUBS AND A PLETHORA
OF SINKS STILL STAND AS
MONUMENTS TO CUBA'S
GRAND NINETEENTH-CENTURY
LIFESTYLE.

OVERLEAF:
FIG. 133. A DINING ROOM IN
THE HOME OF A WEALTHY
TOBACCO PLANTER IN THE
FISHING PORT OF GIBARA,
BELIEVED LOCALLY TO BE THE
SITE OF COLUMBUS'S FIRST
LANDING ON THE ISLAND IN
1492

FIG. 134. A TYPICAL SPANISH
ANTILLEAN TOWNHOUSE
KITCHEN OF THE TYPE BUILT
IN THE SEVENTEENTH AND
EIGHTEENTH CENTURIES.
THE BAROQUE CARVED HOOD
PROVIDED VENTILATION AND
THE MAHOGANY *TINAJERO*
CABINET IN THE FOREGROUND
CONTAINED POROUS JARS FOR
FILTERING WATER, AN ESSEN-
TIAL FOR EVERY KITCHEN.

which water was poured into a large jar beneath, was an essential for townhouse kitchens.

As the demand for the quickly changing revival fashions of the nineteenth century increased, so too did the opening of shops and small furniture factories in Cuba.

Piecework and assembly-line construction became more the rule than the exception in furniture production and the Cuban cabinetmaker began to lose his appreciation for the craft. Furniture-makers who had crafted entire pieces began to specialize in performing specific tasks in an assembly process. As a result, the cabinetmaker was replaced by less talented furniture-makers and apprentices whose goals were efficiency of production rather than quality.

Although this new industrialization fulfilled the needs of an emerging native bourgeoisie, it left the wealthy elite wanting better-quality furniture not available to the middle class.

FIG. 135. A DETAIL OF THE
CARVING ON THE CHAIR
SHOWN IN FIGURE 136

BELOW RIGHT:
FIG. 136. AN INTRICATELY
CARVED CUBAN MAHOGANY
AND CANE ROCKING CHAIR
FROM THE 1860S, FOUND
IN SANTIAGO DE CUBA

OPPOSITE:
FIG. 137. THE SUGAR TRADE
BROUGHT AFFLUENCE TO
CUBA, AND TOWNHOUSES
WERE GRAND AND ELABO-
RATELY FURNISHED, AS IS
THIS ONE IN MATANZAS.

Hence, the Cuban oligarchy began to look elsewhere and import period antiques (particularly French ones) and finer reproduction furniture from North America and Europe. Although fine furniture was imported, Cuban-made furniture never totally lost its appeal to Cuban aristocrats and rooms usually contained a mixture of fashion.

> *Side by side with the numerous pieces of furniture and artifacts that were imported from abroad, it was usual to place other pieces made in Cuba. Cuban furniture is primarily differentiated by its use of the island's native timbers: cedar, ebony, mahogany, rosewood, and others. It includes tried and tested objects of local use, such as rocking chairs, comadritas (armless rockers), tinajeros for water filtering and cooling, and smoking chairs.*[68]

Through the century, island colonial furniture continued to change stylistically as wealthy merchants and landowners imported superior machine-made furniture in the popular styles of the day, as well as period antique furniture from Europe. Examples included Baroque- and Rococo-style carved gilt-wood furniture, painted and gilded Louis XIV-style pieces with marble tops, Napoleon III boulle work, tortoiseshell-marquetry veneered pieces, and Second Empire revival pieces with brass inlay and gilt-bronze mounts. Although island craftsmen continued to make furniture variations of the aforementioned imports, their local pieces were far less grand, constructed and carved from native woods, and therefore better suited to the growing number of the Creole bourgeoisie. Eventually the abundance of imported North American and European revival-style furniture and the numerous island-made copies saturated the colonies and precluded the demand for Spanish colonial furniture.

merchants imported both antiques and contemporary machine-made pieces from Europe.

FIG. 138. THE COURTYARD OF
ONE OF THE MANY PRESTI-
GIOUS RESDENCES IN THE
CUBANCÁN DISTRICT OF
HAVANA IS SURROUNDED BY
A PORTICOED GALLERY WITH
COLUMNS MADE OF DIFFER-
ENT KINDS OF MARBLE.

FIG. 139. THE LATE EIGH-
TEENTH-CENTURY CASA DEL
CONDE DE CASA LOMBILLO
IN HAVANA. IN THE NINE-
TEENTH CENTURY, THE
WOODEN GATES OF THE
LARGER PALACES OF HAVANA
WERE REPLACED WITH DECO-
RATED IRON GRILLES.

FIG. 140. IN A HAVANA HOME,
THESE STAINED-GLASS PANEL
DOORS, TOGETHER WITH
LARGE STAINED-GLASS WIN-
DOWS, ALLOW LIGHT INTO A
RECEPTION ROOM THAT LEADS
ONTO A SMALL COURTYARD.

A traveler to Cuba recorded her impressions of a typical late nineteenth-century Havana home in 1886:

The house forms a great square, and you enter the court, round which are the offices, the rooms for the negroes, coal-house, bath-room, etc., and in the middle of which stands the volantes. Proceed upstairs, and enter a large gallery which runs all round the house. Pass into the Sala, a large cool apartment, with marble floors and tables, and chaise-longues with elastic cushions, chairs, and arm-chairs of cane. A drapery of white muslin and blue silk divides this from a second and smaller drawing-room, now serving as my dressing-room, and beautifully fitted up, with Gothic toilet-table, inlaid mahogany bureau, marble center and side-tables, fine mirrors, cane sofas and chairs, green and gold paper. A drapery of white muslin and rose-colored silk divides this from a bedroom, also fitted up with all manner of elegances. French beds with blue silk coverlids and clear mosquito curtains, and fine lace. A drapery divides this on one side from the gallery; and this room opens into others which run all round the house. The floors are marble or stucco—the roof beams of pale blue wood placed transversely, and the whole has an air of agreeable coolness. Everything is handsome without being gaudy, and admirably adapted for the climate. The sleeping apartments have no windows, and are dark and cool, while the drawing-rooms have large windows down to the floor, with green shutters kept closed till the evening.[69]

From the early colonial days, painted walls had been used in private homes as well as religious and civic buildings, and during the last half of the nineteenth century decorative painting on walls had a resurgence in Cuba. "Even in the 1500s, the New Laws of the Indies dic-

FIG. 143. CUBANS TODAY CONTINUE TO PRACTICE COLONIAL TRADITIONS, ESPECIALLY IN THE PROVINCIAL VILLAGES.

LEFT:
FIG. 142. ONE OF THE RECEPTION ROOMS IN THE LATE SEVENTEENTH-CENTURY CASA DEL CONDE DE BAYONA IN HAVANA, WITH AN OPULENT COLLECTION OF NINETEENTH-CENTURY CUBAN FURNITURE.

OPPOSITE:
FIG. 141. IN THIS RECEPTION ROOM IN THE CASA DEL CONDE DE BAYONA, THE COLORED GLASS *LUCETAS* AND ELABORATE DESIGNS OF THE PANELED CEILING ARE AMONG THE BUILDING'S MOST DECORATIVE ASPECTS.

FIG. 144. THE NEO-MOORISH
PALACIO DEL VALLE IN
CIENFUEGOS, BUILT AT THE
END OF THE NINETEENTH
CENTURY, EXEMPLIFIES THE
MOORISH INFLUENCE THAT
LASTED OVER 400 YEARS OF
CUBAN HISTORY.

FIG. 145. THE INTERIOR OF
THE PALACIO DEL VALLE IN
CIENFUEGOS, WHERE MOROC-
CAN CRAFTSMEN FABRICATED
THE DECORATION

OPPOSITE:
FIG. 146. THIS NINE-
TEENTH-CENTURY CUBAN
CEDAR- AND MAHOGANY-
PANELED PHARMACY IN
MATANZAS WAS FAMILY-
OWNED UNTIL 1964.

LEFT:
FIG. 147. DURING THE
COLONIAL ERA, COLORED
GLASS WAS INTRODUCED,
NOT ONLY TO HELP ILLUMI-
NATE ROOMS, BUT TO
SOFTEN THE BRIGHT TROPI-
CAL SUN. PANELS OF COL-
ORED GLASS, MORE OFTEN
THAN NOT SEMI-CIRCULAR
IN FORM (*MEDIOPUNTOS*),
WERE PLACED ABOVE WIN-
DOWS AND DOORS. THIS
ONE, WHICH FEATURES THE
COLORS OF THE SPANISH
FLAG, IS ABOVE THE
ENTRANCE TO THE
PHARMACY IN MATANZAS
SHOWN OPPOSITE.

BELOW LEFT:
FIG. 148. A LARGE AND
BEAUTIFUL HAND-PAINTED
CERAMIC JAR WITH ITS
ORIGINAL OWNER, THE
FRENCH PHARMACIST
TRIOLET, PICTURED ON THE
FRONT, CAN BE SEEN IN
THE MATANZAS PHARMACY.

tated rich saturated colors for building façades, both to refresh the eye and cut the glare of the sun."[70]

In contrast to the impact of reproduction furniture, decorative wall painting and colorful ornamental ceramic tile imported from Spanish manufacturers were two of the most significant decorative expressions of the late colonial period in Cuba. The art of decorative wall painting was so fully developed that Creole nobility often commissioned professional European fresco artists to do elaborate paintings. In a nineteenth-century travel log, a writer records the colors of a room and its interior:

FIG. 149. THESE DETAILED *MEDIOPUNTOS*, OR FANLIGHTS, WERE DESIGNED TO LIGHT THE ROOM AND THE LOUVERED DOORS TO PROVIDE VENTILATION WHILE SITTERS ROCKED IN THE MAHOGANY AND CANE CHAIRS TO KEEP THEMSELVES COOL.

OPPOSITE:
FIG. 150. FANLIGHTS, KNOWN AS *MEDIOPUNTOS*, WERE DESIGNED TO LIGHT ROOMS THAT OPENED OFF THE CENTRAL ENCLOSED PATIO. THE LOUVERED DOORS PROVIDE VENTILATION.

The window shutters and door are of blue frames and gray panels. The mighty walls are a mournful green with gold molding running around the ceiling and the door and the windows, and separating the corners that are a deeper blue than the great expanse of colors, from the other shade. There are in this enchanted apartment, including the floor, four distinct blues and three greens; and I trace two other blue tints, and crimson and orange, and some specks of rainbow mixture in the spread on the bed, which one is supposed to pull over the knees when midnight cools the air in sultry midwinter! The Spanish yellow predominates in the upper and inner window curtains—but, as they are six feet beyond reach, one does not become familiar with them. There are scarlet trimmings around the canopies of mosquito curtains, that on a steel frame adorned with bronzes and mother-of-pearl, making the bed Oriental, as it were; and the ribbon loops that hold back the gauzy curtains of the bed are vivid crimson. The splendid Spanish arms on broad, golden shields, are at the head and foot of the sumptuous couch; and there are curtains trimmed with lace that hide the legs of the steel bedstead, and have the effect of pantalets.[71]

FIG. 152. THE WOODEN FAN-
LIGHTS AND LOUVERED SHUT-
TERS IN THIS DINING ROOM
PROVIDE LIGHT AND AIR.

OPPOSITE:
FIG. 151. THE DINING ROOM
IN THE EIGHTEENTH-CENTURY
PALACIO DE LOS CAPITÁNES
GENERALES IN HAVANA.
THE MARBLE USED FOR THE
FLOORS IN THE *PALACIO* WAS
IMPORTED FROM ITALY. ON
THE FAR WALL IS AN EIGH-
TEENTH-CENTURY DUTCH
TAPESTRY, "THE BUILDING
OF THE TEMPLE BY KING
SOLOMON."

FIG. 153. A HAVANA DINING
ROOM WITH CUBAN-MADE
FRENCH EMPIRE-STYLE
FURNITURE

OPPOSITE:
FIG. 154. THE DINING
ROOM OF THE PALACIO
DE LA CONDESA DE
REVILLA DE CAMARGO
IN HAVANA

FIG. 155. ONE OF THE MOST
ELABORATELY CARVED CUBAN
PIECES FOUND TO DATE. THIS
NINETEENTH-CENTURY
MAHOGANY EXAMPLE FROM A
HAVANA COLLECTION IS THE
QUINTESSENTIAL CUBAN
ROCOCO REVIVAL PIECE.

OPPOSITE:
FIG. 156. THE HALL AND
GRAND STAIRCASE IN THE
PALACIO DE LA CONDESA DE
REVILLA DE CAMARGO, BUILT
BY WEALTHY PLANTER JOSÉ
GÓMEZ MENA

As Cuban wealth increased, so did the demand for luxurious furniture. At the same time,

the emerging Creole middle class also needed furnishings, although of a less opulent quality.

OPPOSITE:
FIG. 157. AN EIGHTEENTH-CENTURY CREOLE PALACE, THE FORMER HOME OF A TOBACCO-TRADING FAMILY, WITH A SUITE OF CUBAN MAHOGANY AND CANE MEDALLION FURNITURE AND COLORED GLASS *MAMPARAS*

FIG. 158. THE LIBRARY OF A GIBARA HOME, WITH SHELVES FABRICATED FROM ISLAND MAHOGANY

Although wealth continued to increase and the homes of planters, merchants, government officials, and European aristocracy proliferated and became more opulent, and the demand for luxurious furniture also increased, there also emerged a Creole middle class that built smaller houses and required less expensive furniture. To fill this demand, an increasing number of cabinetmakers were employed. Both Spanish and other European immigrants and enslaved and freed African West Indians continued to reinforce their construction techniques, decorative motifs, and integrated designs in this less expensive Cuban furniture. Ultimately, furniture became less elaborate and production steeply declined.

FIG. 159. FRENCH FURNITURE
WAS POPULAR AND INFLU-
ENCED CUBAN CABINETMAK-
ERS PERIODICALLY THROUGH-
OUT THE EIGHTEENTH AND
NINETEENTH CENTURIES.
RATHER THAN USING GILT-
BRONZE OR BRASS FITTINGS,
ISLAND FURNITURE-MAKERS
CARVED THEIR DECORATIVE
MOTIFS DIRECTLY INTO THE
WOOD.

OPPOSITE:
FIG. 160. THE CORNER OF
THIS ROOM IN A PRIVATE NINE-
TEENTH-CENTURY PROVINCIAL
COLONIAL HOME EXEMPLIFIES
ONE OF THE ESSENTIAL INGRE-
DIENTS OF CUBAN ELEGANCE:
ITS SIMPLICITY.

OPPOSITE:
FIG. 161. THE HOME IN
REMEDIOS OF THE LATE
CUBAN MUSICIAN AND COM-
POSER ALEJANDRO GARCIA
CATURIA, WITH ITS BEAUTIFUL
GREEN-TINTED *MAMPARAS*
OPENING ONTO THE PATIO

UPPER LEFT:
FIG. 162. THESE *MAMPARAS*,
OR DOUBLE-SWING HALF-
DOORS, SERVE AS PARTIAL
OUTER DOORS TO PROTECT
PRIVACY WHILE STILL ALLOW-
ING VENTILATION.

LOWER LEFT:
FIG. 163. *MAMPARAS*, OR
GLASSED DOOR-SCREENS,
HELPED TO ESTABLISH
PRIVACY, YET ALLOWED
THE BREEZE TO FLOW
THROUGH.

FIG. 164. A CUBAN MAHOGANY
AND CANE ARMCHAIR FROM
THE LAST DECADE OF THE
NINETEENTH CENTURY, FEA-
TURING AN ART NOUVEAU-
DESIGNED BACK

FIG. 165. A REAR LOGGIA OF
THE PALACIO JUNCO IN
MATANZAS, BUILT BETWEEN
1835 AND 1840. THE RENAIS-
SANCE-REVIVAL MAHOGANY
AND CANE FURNITURE IS
CUBAN-MADE.

FIG. 166. CUBA'S NEOCLASSICAL AND EMPIRE FURNITURE STYLES WERE FOLLOWED BY A HEAVY CLASSICAL-REVIVAL STYLE IN WHICH BOLDLY PROPORTIONED MAHOGANY FURNITURE HAD SCROLLED LEGS, STRAIGHT COLUMNS, AND FLAT SURFACES DEVOID OF CARVING.

FIG. 167. A SECOND-FLOOR DRAWING ROOM IN THE 1830S PALACIO JUNCO IN MATANZAS, FEATURING MID-NINETEENTH- AND EIGHTEENTH-CENTURY CUBAN FURNITURE

OVERLEAF LEFT:
FIG. 168. AN ECLECTIC PRIVATE COLLECTION OF CUBAN AND EUROPEAN PIECES IN TRINIDAD

OVERLEAF RIGHT:
FIG. 169. ANOTHER PRIVATELY OWNED COLLECTION OF NINETEENTH-CENTURY CUBAN FURNITURE AND OBJETS D'ART

The emancipation in 1886 and the continual war for Cuban independence brought about the decline of the sugar economy and the dissolution of the plantocracy. By the turn of the twentieth century, most of the Cuban plantation great houses were fast showing signs of decay. An eyewitness account of Cuba in 1896 states:

> *The once opulent planters of the Island were fond, in the days of pomp, of approaching their country palaces through avenues of royal palms, and now the solemn, neglected trees tell of the glories of these days that are gone.*[72]

Today the Cuban furniture-making tradition is only a shadow of its former self, but the expressions of form created by Cuban cabinetmakers of the past remain a tribute to their skill, versatility, and innovative sense of design. The study of these superb pieces continues to illuminate the creative contributions of Cuban craftsmen and their role in the social and economic history of Cuba, as well as their role in the history of the decorative arts.

CONCLUSION

This book is the first comprehensive investigation and account of the development of Cuban colonial furniture and its makers. It encompasses a wider variety of material than has previously been considered, and presents Cuban furniture as a decorative art form viewed through its historical development. Research for this investigation was challenging for a number of unique reasons. Travel in Cuba is difficult, and is restricted by the United States government as the trade embargo continues. The Archives of the Indies in Seville and the Cuban National Archives and their bureaucracy were also difficult to access. Of the few valuable entries from the Jamaican Archives and the Island Record Office—both in Spanish Town, Jamaica—only inventories and wills were found, which mentioned furniture related to Spanish and Cuban forms. In addition, documentary historical source material for research on Cuban colonial furniture-makers is very rare. Owing to the dearth of written records, there were only a few nineteenth-century pieces for which documented provenance did exist. Therefore, tracing, identifying, and categorizing the development of Cuban furniture had to be done by researching the wood and the construction techniques used, and by stylistic interpretation of the furniture forms themselves. The contribution of both Hispanic-Moorish and African craftsmen to Cuban furniture-making should serve as an inspiration for further study of the confluence of cultures in the colonial era and how it affected the development of the craftsmanship tradition in Cuba.

The strengths of both Hispanic-Moorish and African traditions and influences did not dissipate over the colonial era, but were constantly reinforced by the continual migration of craftsmen from Spain and by the importation of enslaved Africans. The construction, turning, and carving techniques, design patterns, choice of decorative motifs, and exotic native woods all contribute to the cornucopia of design characteristics that define Cuban style. Cuban colonial furniture is a source material for study that provides insight not only into the work of the island artisans, but to the rich history and lifestyle that was Cuba's culture as it was manifested in the art of furniture-making during the colonial era.

In conclusion, the island's colonial furniture, with its ever changing fashions and history, becomes part of Cuba's cultural essence, or *Cubanidad,* by the many different ways the Cuban craftsmen transfigured Spanish, Arabic, African, European, and North American styles into the unique combination of forms that we have today.

FIG. 171. DURING THE NINE-
TEENTH CENTURY, NORTH
AMERICAN AND EUROPEAN
VICTORIAN WICKER FURNI-
TURE WAS IMPORTED BY THE
SHIPLOAD. SHOWN HERE IS
A COLLECTION DISCOVERED
IN HAVANA.

FIG. 172. TWO MAHOGANY
AND CANE CHAIRS MADE
SPECIFICALLY FOR CHILDREN

NOTES

1. Hector Rivero Borrell, M. Gustavo Curiel, Antonio Rubial Garcia, Juana Gutierrez Haces, and David B. Warren, *The Grandeur of Viceregal Mexico: Treasures from the Museo Franz Mayer* (The Museum of Fine Arts, Houston, Museo Franz Mayer, Mexico 2002), 130.

2. Michael Anthony, *The Golden Quest,* (London: Macmillan Press, Ltd., 1992), 33.

3. *Cuba,* (London: Doris Kindersley, 2002 , Penguin Co.), 210.

4. Alec Waugh, *A Family of Islands* (New York: Doubleday & Company, Inc. , 1964), 3.

5. J. H. Parry and P. M. Sherlock, *A Short History of the West Indies,* 2nd ed. (London: Macmillan Press, Ltd., 1963), 11.

6. Bartolomé de las Casas, *Historia de las Indias* (Mexico: Fondo de Cultura Económica, 1951), 6.

7. Eric Williams, *From Columbus to Castro: The History of the Caribbean* (New York: Vintage, 1970), 25.

8. Rachel Carley and Andrea Brizzi, *Cuba: 400 Years of Architecture* (New York: Whitney Library of Design, 1997), 53, 55.

9. Fernando Marais, *The Dictionary of Art,* Vol. 29 (New York: Grove, 1996), 264.

10. Doménech Gallissá Rafael, *Antique Spanish Furniture,* translated from the Spanish by Grace Hardendorf Burr (New York: Archive Press, 1965), 20.

11. Arthur Byne and Mildred Stapley, *Spanish Interiors and Furniture,* Vol. I (New York: William Helburn, Inc.), i.

12. Miles Danby, *Moorish Style* (New York: Phaidon, 1995), 118.

13. María Luisa Lobo Montalvo, *Havana: History and Architecture of a Romantic City* (New York: Monacelli Press, 2000), 45.

14. Ibid., 72.

15. Murat Halstead, *The Story of Cuba, Her Struggles For Liberty* (Chicago: Cuba Libre Publishing Co., 1806), 450–51.

16. R. W. Symonds, "Early Imports of Mahogany Furniture," *The Connoisseur,* Vol. 94, no. 398 (October 1934), 215.

17. Sali Katz, *Hispanic Furniture: An American Collection from the Southwest* (Stamford: Architectural Book Publishing, 1986), 63.

18. Andrew Gravette, *Architectural Heritage of the Caribbean: An A–Z of Historic Buildings* (Princeton: Marcus Weiner Publishers, 2000), 20.

19. Mario Paz Aguiló, *The Dictionary of Art,* Vol. 29 (New York: Grove, 1996), 310.

20. Colin Cooke and Sylvia Shorto, "Some Notes on Early Bermudian Furniture," *Antiques Magazine,* August 1979, 335.

21. Ibid., 320.

22. Bryden Hyde, *Bermuda's Antique Furniture and Silver* (Bermuda: Bermuda National Trust, 1971), 18–19.

23. Ibid.

24. Ernest Cardet, *The Dictionary of Art,* Vol. 8 (New York: Grove, 1996), 235.

25. Katz, op. cit., 63.

26. Joan Sacs, "Spanish Chairs of the Seventeenth and Eighteenth Centuries," *Antiques Magazine,* Vol XII, no. 2, 123.

27. Doménech Gallissá Rafael, *Antique Spanish Furniture,* translated from the Spanish by Grace Hardendorf Burr (New York: Archive Press, 1965), 22.

28. *The Grandeur of Viceregal Mexico,* op. cit., 25.

29. Hugh Thomas, *Cuba or The Pursuit of Freedom* (New York: Da Capo Press, 1998), 22.

30. Carley and Brizzi, op. cit., 75.

31. Cardet, op. cit., 235.

32. Richard S. Dunn, *Sugar and Slaves: The Rise of the Planter Class in the West Indies 1624–1713* (Chapel Hill: The University of North Carolina Press, 1972), 16.

33. Hugh Thomas, *The Slave Trade* (New York: Simon & Schuster, 1997), 91.

34. Ibid, 95.

35. John E. Willis, Jr., *1688: A Global History* (New York: W. W. Norton), 49–50.

36. Eric Williams, *From Columbus to Castro: The History of the Caribbean* (New York: Vintage, 1970), 144.

37. Montalvo, op. cit., 77.

38. Gravette, op cit., 18.

39. J. H. Parry and P. M. Sherlock, *A Short History of the West Indies,* 2nd ed. (London: Macmillan 1963), 71.

40. Ibid., 18.

41. Thomas, *The Slave Trade,* op. cit., 231.

42. *The Grandeur of Viceregal Mexico,* op. cit., 172.

43. Cardet, op. cit., 235.

44. *The Grandeur of Viceregal Mexico,* op. cit., 32.

45. Eric Deschodt and Philippe Morane, *The Cigar* (Köln: Koneman, 1998), 43.

46. Montalvo, op. cit., 77.

47. Gary R. Libby, *Cuba: A History in Art* (Daytona Beach: The Museum of Arts and Sciences, 1997), 13–14.

48. Montalvo, op. cit., 72.

49. Sherry Johnson, *The Social*

Transformation of Eighteenth-Century Cuba (Florida, University Press of Florida, 2001), 10.

50. Cardet, op. cit., 235.

51. R.W. Symonds, "English Eighteenth Century Furniture Exports to Spain and Portugal," *The Burlington Magazine* Vol. XXViii, (1941).

52. Doménech Gallissá Rafael, *Antique Spanish Furniture,* translated from the Spanish by Grace Hardendorf Burr (New York: Archive Press, 1965), 20.

53. Cardet, op. cit., 35.

54. Ibid.

55. Ibid.

56. Susan R. Stein, *The Worlds of Thomas Jefferson at Monticello* (New York: Harry N. Abrams, Inc., 1993), 280.

57. Cybele Trione Gontar, *The Louisiana Campeche Chair: Origin, History and Transference* (unpublished Thesis), 23.

58. Montalvo, op. cit., 118.

59. Thomas, *Cuba,* op. cit., 77.

60. Montalvo, op. cit., 120.

61. Ibid., 121.

62. Nancy McClelland, *Duncan Phyfe and the English Regency: 1795–1830* (New York: William R. Scott, Inc., 1939; reprint, New York: Dover, 1980), 196.

63. Llilian Llanes, *The Houses of Old Cuba* (New York: Thames and Hudson, 1999), 155.

64. Adolfo De Hostos, *Historia de San Juan, ciudad murado: ensayo acerca del proceso del proceso de la civiizaciaon en la ciudad Espanola de San Juan Bautista de Puerto Rico, 1521–1898* (Puerto Rico: Instituto de Cultura Puertorriqueana, 1966), 519–21.

65. Montalvo, op. cit., 121.

66. De Hostos, op. cit.

67. Many advertisements appeared in Cuban newspapers announcing the arrival of ships from the north with cargoes of furniture. The low price of imported furniture inevitably accelerated demand, and this factor had a powerful influence on Cuban craftsmanship; spectacular items of carved and inlaid furniture were produced as the industry expanded and diversified. See Cardet, op. cit., 235.

68. Montalvo, op. cit.

69. Frances Calderón de la Barca, *Life in Mexico* (Berkley and Los Angeles: University of California Press, 1982), 21–22.

70. Carley and Brizzi, op. cit., 125–27.

71. Halstead, op. cit., 19.

72. Ibid., 166.

ACKNOWLEDGMENTS

I count it an honor to have been able to research and write this book in Cuba. During my explorations and study of colonial Cuba I felt like an anachronism, that is, I felt out of time, as if I had stepped back into history and had literally become part of the colonial era. Because of the preservation of Cuba's architecture, fine and decorative arts, customs, and traditions—sometimes preserved by neglect and often by splendid restoration and conservation—I was fortunate to experience a country uncluttered by random destruction of its patrimony, which made my job of recording Cuba's colonial centuries of furniture an exciting process of discovery.

None of this would have been possible without the help of Maria de Lourdes (Luly) Duke, a Cuban-American who is president and founder of Fundación Amistad. She opened many doors in Cuba, some of which had been closed since the revolution in the late 1950s, and made introductions to decorative arts scholars who have never been outside the country.

Among the many other people I want to thank for their invaluable information, resources and help are Marta Arjona Pérez, Presidenta Consejo Nacional de Patrimonio Cultural; Eusebio Leal Spengler, Historiador de la Ciudad de la Habana; Rafael Rojas Hurtado de Mendoza, Director del Plan Maestro de Revitalización Integral de la Habana Vieja, Oficina del Historiador de la Ciudad;

Marcia Leiseca; Patricia Semidey; Celene Valcálcer; Alicia García Santana; Severino Rodríguez; José Linares; Raida Mara Suárez, Portal Directora de Patrimonio, Oficina del Historiador de la Ciudad de la Habana; Margarita Suárez García, Directora de la Museo de Arte Colonial; Marta Castellaños Bosch; Argel Calcines; Robert and Sharon Bartos; Emilio Cueto; and Leslie Knowlton.

I would also like to express my heartfelt thanks to Bruce Buck, absolutely the best interiors photographer there is, and Trudy Rosato, my business partner at Connors Rosato Gallery in New York City, whose scholarly editing of this manuscript and sole management of our gallery while I was in Cuba made this book possible.

I am also indebted to the terrific team I worked with at Harry N. Abrams: Eric Himmel, the editor-in-chief, who first believed in my project; Elaine Stainton, my editor, who patiently and tirelessly worked on the text; and Robert McKee, the designer, whose vision helped recreate the colonial elegance on the page.

Finally, I express my deepest gratitude to the Cuban people. I have made friendships in Cuba that will last a lifetime and sincerely hope that this book will not only contribute to the recognition of Cuban colonial furniture and its furniture makers but also serve to encourage further research and conservation of this important part of Cuba's patrimony.

Michael Connors

Editor: Elaine M. Stainton
Designer: Robert McKee
Production Manager: Jane G. Searle

Library of Congress Cataloging-in-Publication Data
Connors, Michael
 Cuban elegance / by Michael Connors;
photographs by Bruce Buck.
  p. cm.
Includes bibliographical references and index.
 ISBN 0–8109–4337–9
 1. Furniture design—Cuba.
2. Furniture, Colonial—Cuba. I. Title.
 NK2474.C66 2004
 749'.097291—dc22
                              2003020924

Harry N. Abrams, Inc.
100 Fifth Avenue
New York, N.Y. 10011
www.abramsbooks.com

Abrams is a subsidiary of

LA MARTINIÈRE GROUPE